BENEFAC

JOSHUA BIRKHOLZ + AMY LAMPI

BENEFACTORS
WHY SOME FUNDRAISING PROFESSIONALS ALWAYS SUCCEED

Foreword by Kevin J. Foyle, MBA, CFRE
Chair, Association of Fundraising Professionals Global Board

WILEY

Library of Congress Cataloging-in-Publication Data:
Names: Birkholz, Joshua, author. | Lampi, Amy, author.
Title: Benefactors : fundraising strategies for the 21st century / Joshua
   Birkholz, Amy Lampi.
Description: First edition. | Hoboken, NJ : Wiley, [2023] | Includes index.
Identifiers: LCCN 2022027220 (print) | LCCN 2022027221 (ebook) | ISBN
   9781119932796 (hardback) | ISBN 9781119932819 (adobe pdf) | ISBN
   9781119932802 (epub)
Subjects: LCSH: Fund raising.
Classification: LCC HG177 .B485 2023 (print) | LCC HG177 (ebook) | DDC
   361.7068/1—dc23/eng/20220809
LC record available at https://lccn.loc.gov/2022027220
LC ebook record available at https://lccn.loc.gov/2022027221

Cover Design: Wiley
Cover Image: © Macrovector/Shutterstock;
Devita ayu silvianingtyas/Shutterstock

SKY10035838_082422

To you, the new fundraiser about to experience first-hand the transformation possible through generosity, and to the seasoned professional, perhaps tired, weary, and persevering through an era of change—this book is for you. May we come together to encourage and uplift each other in gratitude and camaraderie to be the best agents of philanthropy that we can possibly be.

FOREWORD

I have enjoyed getting to know Josh Birkholz and Amy Lampi over the past several years through consulting, volunteer projects, and speaking engagements with the University of Texas System and the Association of Fundraising Professionals. Therefore, I was honored to partner with them on their next project, *BeneFactors*.

As fundraising innovators, Josh and Amy saw the need years ago for equipping the next generation of fundraisers and nonprofit leaders for a modern approach to fundraising. Historically, most professionals "fell into the field" of fundraising—and there remains to be seen a comprehensive primer currently in the market of what attributes or "factors" make up the modern fundraiser. That is why I think this new resource will be a benefit for our sector as it moves forward in what remains uncertain times. It is now more critical than ever that fundraisers understand the soft skills needed to develop into the nonprofit leaders of today and tomorrow.

As advancement leaders, we were seeing a talent crisis on the horizon even prior to the pandemic, but we did not realize how much the pandemic would exacerbate the shortage of qualified professionals in our field. It is estimated that thousands of development professionals left the field during the pandemic, leaving an even wider chasm of positions to fill in the nonprofit sector. I currently serve as board chair for the Association of Fundraising Professionals (AFP), a global organization consisting of 26,000 members in more than 240 chapters throughout the world. At AFP, we anticipate 80,000+ leaders to exit the nonprofit sector annually as the Baby Boomer generation retires. Why is this important? Nearly one million leaders will be leaving our sector over the next decade who are responsible for facilitating hundreds of billions of contributed revenue dollars to the US economy. According to *Giving USA 2022: The Annual Report on Philanthropy*, giving reached a record high of $484.85 billion in 2021 as we continued to navigate the pandemic. If equipped with the skills necessary, I strongly believe that fundraising professionals are uniquely positioned to be the leaders of our future nonprofits as we continue to elevate and empower philanthropy in our society.

However, we must start early and think big: What if every student leaving college or university knew what the development profession is and can make an informed choice to enter the field? I join Josh and Amy in wanting *BeneFactors* to not only inspire the emerging or current fundraising leader, but also to provide a practical guide for academic philanthropy programs on our university campuses across the nation.

Please join me, Josh, and Amy in advancing our field for the fundraising professionals and leaders of tomorrow.

Kevin J. Foyle, MBA, CFRE
Chair, Association of Fundraising
Professionals Global Board
Senior Vice President for Development & Public Affairs
UTHealth Houston

CONTENTS

After years of discussion and refinement, we settled on eight key characteristics, or factors, of the modern fundraiser. We believe these characteristics distinguish the greatest fundraisers from all who have gone before, and then we used those traits to fashion these concepts into persona-based chapters.

Is the growing emphasis on data science and predictive analytics a threat to the relationship builder? How might a frontline officer embrace data as an asset for building stronger relationships with the right people and the right things? Expect a practical understanding of data and decision science with nonthreatening practical applications.

embracing this change. From prospecting to warming, and from donor experience management to direct relationship building, the digital and social landscape presents new opportunities for the astute fundraiser.

ACKNOWLEDGMENTS

We would like to first extend gratitude to our spouses (Tracy and PJ) and daughters (Zoe, Nora, Charis, Emily, and Lauren) for allowing us to take time away from our families to write this book and for their constant dedication and support as we continue to pursue this all-encompassing profession of philanthropy. We would also like to thank our colleagues at BWF who have given of their time and expertise to help make this book a reality, especially Carole Arwidson, Meredith Berry, Allison Gannon, Justin Ware, Alex Oftelie, Bond Lammey, and Betsy Rigby. We are sincerely appreciative of Kevin Foyle for his contribution of the Foreword; and are grateful to our friends and colleagues in the profession who were contributors or provided support or endorsements for the book: Greg Robertson, Vu Le, Loubel Galik, Kristen Schlatre, Andrea Soper, Amir Pasic, Kathryn Van Sickle, Laura MacDonald, Victor Yates, and Andrew Recinos. Lastly, we would like to thank Brian Neill, Deborah Schindlar, and all our friends at Wiley for believing in this book and entrusting us with their resources.

And now abideth faith, hope, charity, these three; but the greatest of these is charity.

—1 Corinthians 13:13 KJV

ABOUT THE AUTHORS

Josh Birkholz is the CEO of the international fundraising services firm BWF. Josh is a leader in big philanthropy and an innovator in the business of fundraising. In his nearly two decades of consulting with leading nonprofits, universities, and healthcare centers around the world, Josh has redefined how we look at modern program design, fundraising in an evolving economy, and positioning in the high-net-worth marketplace.

Josh is the author of *Fundraising Analytics: Using Data to Guide Strategy* (Wiley, 2008) and a contributor to the books *A Kaleidoscope of Prospect Development* (CASE, 2008) and *Return on Character* (Harvard Business Review Press, 2015). In his roles as chair of the Advisory Council on Methodology, vice chair, and now chair of the board for the Giving USA Foundation, he has informed the Giving USA annual books since 2014. Among his awards for fundraising innovation, he received the Crystal Apple Award from CASE and the Apra Visionary award for his contributions to prospect development.

Amy Lampi is an associate vice president at BWF with more than 20 years of fundraising experience in the performing arts, education, and healthcare. As a development generalist, she has a wide range of experience from multichannel annual giving and development operations to major gifts and management of a development team. Prior to BWF, Amy held development leadership positions in the performing arts, where her cutting-edge work in fundraising analytics with Josh Birkholz of BWF was featured in the August 2016 issue of *The Chronicle of Philanthropy*. She is a recognized national leader and speaker within the Tessitura Network and AFP as well as in her home-town of Houston. She is the immediate past president of AFP Greater Houston Chapter and serves on the AFP LEAD 2022 conference committee. Amy lectures on donor relations and fundraising analytics for Rice University's Glasscock School of Continuing Studies.

INTRODUCTION

Amy and I love fundraising. It is not just a job. It is not creepy or weird to ask people for money. It is not our fallback profession.

We have the privilege of seeing people do what they consider to be the most significant achievements of their lifetimes. We are witnesses of true selflessness. We are on the frontlines of what is good about humanity. We are in the business of helping others. We help make the world a better place.

In any other context, this would be hyperbole. In fundraising, it is real. It is palpable. It is inspiring.

But fundraising is also a tremendous responsibility. Donors let us in through locked doors to their finances, their values, their family, and their deepest passions. The objective of our work means kids can go to school, the environment can be protected, the sick will receive critical care, creativity will advance the human condition, and the hungry can eat. Fundraisers catalyze the generosity that solves the world's problems.

To meet this responsibility, our profession has evolved. Nonprofits today are more professional, systematic, complex, and effective than ever. Campaigns continue to grow to unimaginable levels. As the industry changes, roles in the development operation narrow with ever-increasing specialization. We discuss concepts of scale, sustainable growth, decision science, digital platform marketing, economic forecasting, and talent development. Fundraising will always involve meeting with donors and asking for money. But it is no longer about only that. It is about so much more.

Amy and I have a history of collaboration, including the August 2016 *Chronicle of Philanthropy* cover story in which we provided new methodology for dynamic arts patron identification. We are both proud of our impact on the arts. Today we are focusing our collaborative energy on making a broader impact.

When we contemplated what it means to be modern fundraisers, we realized that we need to be so much more. There is plenty of literature on the craft of asking for money or on specialty areas of fundraising operations. But we've seen relatively little written about the full complement of skills and perspectives the modern fundraiser must possess. Our goal was to push the dialogue about this forward.

Amy and I took a different approach in writing this book than other offerings to the sector. For each attribute we believe an exemplary fundraiser must embody, I identified the concepts and described the essential characteristics. As a longtime consultant to the fundraising profession, I am privileged to have a broad view of many contexts in higher education, healthcare, human services, relief and development, the arts, and the environment—both in the United States and around the world. I get to see first-hand what has worked and what hasn't. At times in this book I reference research studies, proprietary client-based research, or qualitative observation that shaped my thinking. My goal is to present clear theory in a relevant context.

Amy then responds to each concept. As a very successful fundraiser herself with a track record of success in these key components, her goal is to make it real for you. She is the voice of grounded reality to balance my aspirational thinking. By presenting an experienced practitioner's perspective, Amy moved the content from theory into practice.

We encourage you to use this book as a teaching tool for your organization or talent development program. To make this easier for you, Amy provides a discussion guide at the end of each chapter that includes guided discussions to help reinforce the learnings for you and your colleagues.

By no means are the components of *BeneFactors* the final word. Instead, we are proposing a starting point for continued discussion and evolution. Take our book and dissect it. Challenge what needs to be challenged. Promote what warrants promoting. Open your mind to new perspectives, and then test them against your own contexts. Write the next book, blog post, or conference presentation that takes our concepts even further. Our motivation is one of generosity, borne of a desire to share and make you even more effective.

Thank you for choosing the life of a fundraiser. You provide a valuable and meaningful impact in our communities and on the greater world. If you are new to the profession, get ready for an amazing ride. Your donors will be some of the most remarkable people you ever meet. You will see them at their best, and you will help them be their best. If you are a seasoned veteran, thanks for continuing to push yourself with new insights. To everyone, I hope we provide value for the time you give us.

—**Josh Birkholz**

THE DATA-DRIVEN FACTOR

Fundraising will always require sitting in someone's living room and asking for money. Data science helps determine which living rooms to visit.

L et's start with a total cliché. There are two kinds of fundraisers: the *artist* and the *scientist*.

Ugh. I expect you hear this at pretty much every fundraising conference. Some will say these two descriptors exemplify the best mix for a fundraiser. The so-called artist is the relationship builder, whereas the scientist likes to use data. Is this really the best way to describe the professionals in the industry? Is artistry synonymous with relationship building? Is relationship building truly the antithesis of data? Can one not research relationship building like a scientist? Do artists not look at data? Is it really helpful to remind an operations or data professional that *fundraising is really all about relationships*? Are these characteristics mutually exclusive?

I might challenge this dichotomy by considering a really great artist. Take, for example, the concertmaster at your local professional orchestra. This highly regarded position is the first chair violinist entering the stage immediately before the conductor. Certainly, she would qualify as an amazing artist in her own right. How did she achieve such a status? Perhaps it was artistic intuition. Perhaps she studied—a lot. I suspect the latter.

Most likely, this concertmaster began learning the violin at a very young age. She spent many hours a day at home or in a practice room refining her technique. She studied music theory at university to understand harmonic structures, forms, and historic nomenclature. A working knowledge of Italian was necessary for playing under many different conductors. In her deep score study, she realizes that one composer might mean an entirely different thing in using the same marking as another composer. It would not surprise me if she studied wood grains, bow hair, and historic violin makers; can describe the effects of humidity on her instrument; and knows several modern luthiers on a first name basis.

In this situation, would you tell the premier performer that violin is just about playing beautiful music? I might suggest that great artists achieve virtuosity not from intuition or an innate sense of artistry. Rather, they achieve their success through a passionate, resolute commitment to researching and practicing their craft.

Now consider the virtuoso of fundraising. Perhaps she just has an innate talent for asking. Or, perhaps, she studied and practiced over many years. I suspect the latter.

Most likely, this virtuoso fundraiser began as a junior gift officer and faced the same rejection all too common in this profession. Maybe she reached out to an accomplished mentor figure for advice. She took courses on deferred and outright gift options to add to her tool kit. She met with her prospect research professional to learn about asset liquidity and stage-of-life considerations. Over the years, she read books about donor relations, prospect development, metrics approaches, and making asks. She has a history of telling faculty, program officers, or doctors that their pet programs did not test well in a feasibility study. It would not surprise me if she knows several foundation leaders, trust officers, and financial advisors by name.

In this situation, would you tell her that fundraising is just about the art of relationship building? I might suggest that great fundraisers achieve virtuosity not from intuition or an innate sense of artistry. Rather, they achieve their success through a passionate, resolute commitment to researching and practicing their craft.

Logically, the opening premise renders the title of this chapter irrelevant. A data-driven fundraiser is really just a fundraiser. Or maybe not just a fundraiser, but a great fundraiser! Not sold? Okay, let's unpack this a bit.

GROWTH OF DATA SCIENCE

Over the past two decades, all industries witnessed a data science transformation. From predicting shopping patterns to predicting elections, from manipulating shopping patterns to manipulating elections—we've really seen it all. Data is everywhere. Some of it is very cool. Some of it is thoroughly scary. Some businesses are highly ethical and deeply committed to the public good. Some businesses are completely profit-dominated. Automation is welcomed in faster shopping and better playlists. Automation is not so fun if our jobs are on the line. The good, the bad, and the ugly are all tied up into this thing called "data."

In the fundraising profession, we saw the origin in prospect identification. Borrowing from the underwriting book in lending, we produced scores to predict who might be good prospects for future gifts. This was all well and good as long as it remained the purview of the researchers. But then, annual giving and direct marketing programs started to take notice. *Audience personas* and *segmentation* became common nomenclature. This was all well and good as long as it remained the purview of the marketing types. But then, leadership started running capacity analyses and staffing studies for campaigns. Prospect management teams began studying which activities were most influential in closing gifts. Consultants started conducting donor sentiment analysis studies. Now, this was just too close. Fundraisers everywhere began asking themselves "might I be data-d" out of a job? If I am a fundraiser who doesn't understand data, am I truly relevant anymore?"

For me, this line of thinking is completely off the mark. Rather, the value of a great fundraiser is so high that data science is its Fort Knox. Prospecting analytics developed to provide better names. Marketing analytics developed to warm the pipeline and increase the flow. Leadership used the staffing studies and capacity analysis to make the case for more fundraisers. Prospect management teams wanted nothing more than success from the fundraiser. Consultants wanted to tell you what the donors think so you could refine your skills. This data is for you. If you are a fundraiser, committed to your craft, you are truly relevant. Not only that; you are prized.

This fear of professional relevance is the main driver behind the "art and science" discourse. By lumping the hard stuff into a straw man called "science," one can remain relevant by offering the "art." But there isn't anything to fear. Let's look more closely at the science aspect.

PREDICTIVE MODELING

If you were a fundraiser in a one-person shop, surely you needed to find some prospects. Likely you started with your board members and existing donors. You met with the donors giving the most to try and upgrade them to even higher levels. Then the needs expanded and your team grew. To find enough prospects for the campaign, you had to look beyond existing gift levels. To start, you may have screened the file for wealth information.

Your prospects consisted of bigger donors and high-capacity folks regardless of gift history. As the file grew, the pipeline began to overwhelm the fundraiser. High-capacity prospects might have little engagement with the organization, resulting in dead-ends. In response, your researchers studied markers of engagement and produced a simple score to help prioritize the modest donors. Over time, the program continued to grow, and the campaign goals seemed unachievable. With the limitations of public wealth data, how was a fundraiser to find enough prospects? Could we screen for other factors such as probability to give a major gift? This demand saw the birth of predictive modeling for fundraising.

But what is it? At its core and as it pertains to prospecting, predictive modeling is finding distinguishing characteristics of major donors and scoring constituents by their fit to these characteristics. By contrast, market research looks for descriptive characteristics of major donors. Distinction helps you find; description helps you group.

If I were describing the *Where's Waldo* children's book (*Where's Wally* in some countries), I might say it is an illustrated book. It contains very detailed drawings with bright colors. The characters are simple, but the volume of characters and situations make it complex. The idea is to find the namesake character. This description is very accurate.

By contrast, if I were instructing a reader in finding Waldo, I might show a picture and identify his distinguishing characteristics. Waldo wears a red and white striped shirt and a stocking cap. He is rather tall and rail thin. His bangs feather out from under his cap, and he wears round, John Lennon-like glasses. The idea here is to contrast Waldo's characteristics from the other characters on the page. By finding red-and-white-striped shirts on the page, the seeker is more likely to ultimately find Waldo.

Similarly, a predictive model for major donors will not describe characteristics of the donors in a way that enables effective marketing. For example, 75% of major donors might live in the suburbs. This descriptive information might be helpful to marketing in event location planning. However, it might also be true that 75% of constituents in the database live in the suburbs. It gets you no closer to finding a major donor. Rather, it is like describing Waldo to a young reader as a brightly colored cartoon drawing, which does not distinguish him in any meaningful way.

A predictive model will look for differences between major donors and the random population. When these differences emerge, finding more major donors becomes more efficient. An assortment of distinguishing characteristics are assembled into a score. Those with higher scores are more distinct from the random group. Those with lower scores look more like everyone else. By focusing on those with higher scores, the odds of finding a future major donor increase just like looking for the red-and-white-striped shirt helps us find Waldo in a crowd.

In recent years, these scores moved from a static snapshot of distinction to a more dynamic measure. As the data profile of each constituent changed, so too changed their score. In a few cases, organizations are letting statistical software or coding learn and change its criteria without human-driven comparison analysis. This "machine learning" is often called "artificial intelligence." The result is the same insofar as identifying the constituents with the greatest odds of giving a major gift.

Recently, there has been a flood of artificial intelligence solutions for prospecting. With the maturity of the prospect development profession and the vendors that support this part of the sector, the ability to find potential prospects has matured beyond the ability to cultivate all the names to implement. So data sciences began to turn their sights to relationship management.

Predictive modeling for relationship modeling maintains its basis in comparison. However, rather than distinguish which prospects are most likely to give, these models focus on which activities are most likely to lead to gifts. A method used at many larger major gift programs is comparative performance analysis. Fundraisers with the highest levels of production are compared to those with lower production. The characteristics under evaluation are activity data such as visit count, portfolio penetration, visit spacing, time from assignment to first contact, ask levels respective of capacity, ask volume, ask penetration, channel of discovery attempts, number of discovery attempts, cultivation pacing, ask timing, and so on. If the activity under review has the same counts between the two groups, the activity is not a contributing factor for higher production. If the activity measurement is different between the groups, then there is reason for further investigation.

The goal of this type of analysis is not to evaluate the fundraiser, but rather to provide a better route to success. Much like how a GPS provides the best route based on the data at hand, relationship modeling reveals the optimal activities for successful fundraising. The GPS may not know of a new roadblock requiring a revised route. Similarly, relationship modeling simply provides a route subject to revision. Collectively, if the recommended activities influence officer-metric weighting, then the result should be increased production effectiveness by the fundraising team.

Example

Premise: A major US university needed to refine its fundraiser metrics to meet an aggressive major gift campaign goal. Based on existing run rates, it was unlikely to meet the numbers unless a few transformational gifts emerged. The top prospects for the campaign were already solicited. Waiting for unicorn gifts was insufficient.

What They Did: The development program contracted a data scientist to find 20% more production from its major gift team. The data scientist evaluated portfolio composition, performance activities, staff composition, and staffing levels. He conducted a relationship model to determine the top drivers of production. He recommended a shift in focus to solicitation volume with ask-level management at the officer level. He also pointed out that first- and second-year fundraisers were all over the map in solicitation level and timing. He recommended purposeful mentorship in solicitation effectiveness. Thirdly, he recommended a staff ramp-up in select units where there were many highly engaged prospects without manager attention.

The Result: The ramp-up for new fundraisers shortened, production per officer increased, and boldness in asking was met with boldness in giving. The fundraisers were still meeting with prospects as before. However, they were more focused on activities leading to effective solicitations. In short, the fundraisers met their goals. They were data-driven. The data was there to help them. And it did.

CAPACITY ANALYSIS

Historically, as organizations prepared for campaigns, levels were set and fundraising initiatives were prioritized with a feasibility study. A consultant would meet with the top donors to the institution to conduct qualitative interviews. Because big donors primarily determined the success of a campaign, these studies tended to adequately achieve the aims of the campaign. Feasibility studies were, however, inadequate in predicting new donors emerging during the campaign period. And as campaign sizes grew and priorities expanded in breadth, feasibility studies decreased in adequacy. Talking to the best donors continues to provide political, cultivation, and outlier inclusivity value, but they are no longer enough for planning and sizing campaigns.

Data science rose to prominence in providing much needed decision support. Analysts, primarily in the consulting profession, began to evaluate the total of capacity ratings by constituents compared to likelihood and warmth measures. Highly engaged segments would yield a higher share of wallet than colder segments. Mathematically, it was possible to determine how much the file could give based on existing engagement levels. Furthermore, these analysts evaluated the reach of each fundraiser to determine the likely organizational yield. Then, they simulated how much more could be raised by cultivating different constituents, improving performance maximums with relationship modeling, and adding staff members. Now, it was possible to forecast how much might be raised doing business as usual versus how much might be raised by changing up some things a bit.

With ever-increasing pressure to raise more money, chief fundraisers need viable pathways to be successful. No longer can a fundraising executive say to her CEO or board, "We will double our efforts; this is where the rubber meets the road." The risk is too high, and the need for an actual path forward is critical. With a capacity analysis, a fundraising leader can say, with confidence, "With existing staff, it will take X years to achieve this goal. But with investment in staffing and process redesign, we can raise the goal in Y years."

SOURCE AND JOURNEY

In recent years, many data scientists have shifted their attention to journey mapping. The relationship between constituent and organization is long and complex. For many sectors, the relationship begins long before the donor is on the radar of the fundraisers.

In a performing arts organization, for example, a child may attend a school field trip to the theater. Later, she may go with her family to a holiday show. At some point as an adult, she is invited to a performance and has a memorable experience. She may begin to go more regularly. As she succeeds in her business, she may decide to use some of her entertainment budget for a subscription. Through the communications, she learns about a program in the schools. Because of her nostalgia for her first field trip experience, she donates to the program.

The theater continues to delight her with messages of impact in the community. Her giving grows and her relationship deepens. A prospect researcher recognizes she is a successful businesswoman and refers her to a major gift officer. The major gift officer invites her to coffee to talk about her experience. Over time, she grows more passionate about the education program and makes a pledge to support broadening educational accessibility. After many years of continued support, she decides to leave a legacy gift in her estate to endow the head of education programming.

If the pathway to major philanthropy may take a lifetime, it is in the interest of development to understand the journey. Were there moments where a nudge from the organization accelerated giving? Were there experiences that lead to deepened engagement? Are people paying attention to the same channels that used to convert members to donors? This is the root of source and journey analysis.

An analyst might evaluate key sources such as first constituent experience (student, patient, child participant), first donor experience (event, direct response, passive envelope, self-identified), and first personal interaction (discovery visit, event table, called for help with a gift designation). She will also evaluate key journey markers such as patient experiences, shows attended, reunions attended, event participation, outbound appeals, inbound communications, visits, contact reports, solicitations, and so forth. These sources and journeys are compared to measures of lifetime value, or how much a donor will give over their lifetime. Using principles of comparative analysis, she will determine if certain origin points or sequences of events lead to higher lifetime values. She may also evaluate if these changed in recent years compared to past years. For instance, perhaps direct mail was a more effective original source of future major donors, but now the value is more consistent with midlevel lifetime unrestricted support.

For a fundraiser, the analysis may provide guidance for the most effective time or manner to make a discovery visit. The historic map might provide insight about potential designations. The analysis might suggest where to invest the most budget for pipeline development or base giving. Further, the journey map might suggest an optimal cultivation path to match the donors' pacing and objectives.

The main obstacle to source and journey analysis is having enough data. Until recently, many institutions maintained very siloed databases for each area managing a slice of the journey. As enterprise CRM solutions and integrated data warehouses emerged, more of the data became available to the analyst.

Data Visualization

If you are an executive in a fundraising organization, no doubt you have had requests for data visualization software come across your desk. Requests for tools such as Tableau, Advisor, and Qlik are not simply "data people wanting new toys." These represent a very earnest effort to break down the barriers of data for the fundraisers.

Data for data's sake requires no communication. Whether business users understand the analysis would be irrelevant. Data for the sake of improving a program requires communication. It used to be said that statisticians achieved job security through confusing terminology. No longer is this the case. Too many of the brightest analytics professionals were moved out of institutions because of failures to communicate. Let's face it, statistics are not only difficult to explain to nonstatisticians; they are downright boring.

Any semiotics professor would jump at the opportunity to show the efficacy of symbols and context. For example, the color red is often associated with stop because of traffic lights and stop signs. Red dots by a name on a list suggest a less than ideal candidate. The red color carries powerful symbolic weighting. And context is important. Scoring 85 points at the basketball game is only meaningful if you also know the score of the opposing team.

In data visualization, symbolism and context enable nonverbal communication. Using green icons for fundraiser meeting goals, yellow for nearly meeting them, and red for missing goals provides a quick status update of the team's efforts for the fundraising manager. A fundraiser making 15 solicitations, 85 visits, and raising $1.5 million may consider the numbers differently if the higher producers had fewer visits but more asks. He might focus his cultivation visits to be more directed toward timely solicitations.

How data is communicated may be more effective for behavioral change than the data itself. This is why data teams are so enthused about visualization tools. When the findings are clear, contextualized, and consumable, the recipient can understand and calibrate without a lot of explanation. In some cases, the visualization may even be motivating to the recipient. A helpful mnemonic for effective visualization leading to self-governing behavioral change is the word "COAST":

Comparison: Provide context by comparing segments, time periods, or officers.

One idea at a time: Express one key finding you wish to convey.

Alignment: Be sure the data is relevant to the intended recipient.

Simplest form: Complexity might look cool, but it is less effective.

Transparency: Show where people stand without shaming.

TALENT ANALYTICS

To date, most of the data science has lived in two main camps: (1) *Who we fundraise from* (prospecting, segmentation, descriptive analysis, and automated modeling), and (2) *How we fundraise* (relationship modeling, source and journey analysis, and capacity analysis).

Who does the fundraising is an emerging area of research and science. With an ever-expanding need for fundraisers and a talent pool failing to keep pace, talent analysis is more urgent than ever. Although capacity analysis evaluates staffing levels, there is much need for defining characteristics of future talent. This book, for example, seeks to set the stage for deeper analysis into the distinguishing characteristics of great fundraisers.

The danger in talent analytics is to focus on what people *are* rather than what people *do*. Demographics and descriptors are quite subject to biases. Behavioral analysis is not only less subject to bias, it is more productive in application. If certain skills or work habits better distinguish between effective or ineffective fundraisers, then a fundraiser can seek to learn and adopt them. Furthermore, it is more effective for hiring managers to understand the key skills and activities most relevant to the position descriptions.

REJECT THE CLICHÉ

Being a fundraiser does not require you to be a data scientist. But being a data-driven fundraiser acknowledges that data science is beneficial to you. Being a great fundraiser does suggest a passionate commitment to craft. This is a different kind of science, but one every fundraiser can achieve. Like the concert master's dedicated study, research, and practice, you too can commit energy to self-improvement.

DATA IS THE NEW BACON

Any book Josh and I write must start with data. It's not just because we are big data nerds, but because data-driven fundraising works. It raises more money, it saves organizations hours of time, and it is the future of our industry. I am so passionate about data-driven fundraising because it acts as a guide for smart and effective decision-making.

Big Data and analytics are hot topics in many industries these days. All business sectors are employing teams of analysts to achieve efficiency and revenue results. I know this firsthand because my husband is an analytics director managing over 30 employees whose sole responsibility is analytics and reporting for a large healthcare system. The dashboards his team developed for the system have been critical decision-making tools for the institution as they navigate the pandemic. Companies have been using analytics every day to make informed decisions. It is imperative that nonprofit institutions do the same or they will be left behind.

Analytics are everywhere. To prove it, a leading data visualization software, Tableau (with clients across the globe), has an annual conferences with over 100K attendees. A popular entertainment streaming service used analytics to create a binge-watching TV show based on a British TV series. A nationwide electronics company used sensors in the floor in several of its stores to track foot patterns and thereby charge vendors more for its more popular displays. A man walked into a nationwide retailer complaining that his 16-year-old daughter was receiving pregnancy coupons. Based on analytics, the daughter was exhibiting buying patterns of a customer who was pregnant. It winds up that the daughter was indeed pregnant; the retailer knew before the father did.

Now that we have access to data and the tools needed to analyze it, it is more important than ever that we as fundraisers take these next practices, understand them, and implement them.

MY LIFELONG LOVE OF DATA

I suppose I have never shied away from data. I was good at math in school, placing out of it in college. In my career, I came up through the ranks of development operations and individual giving. I started my career in fundraising as a development associate at a regional theater in Silicon Valley.

They sent me to Raiser's Edge software training my first week on the job, so data has always been a part of fundraising for me. I experienced their database conversion from a home-grown MS-DOS custom database that showed "*****" in the amount field when the donor's gift was in the six figures, so converting to RE was a dream. It was user-friendly and the Cadillac of fundraising software.

In each of my positions, I would wield the fundraising database and make it do things I needed as a fundraiser to be successful. The goal was always to use the database to its maximum capabilities because we were paying so much for it as an organization. Process improvement was always key. For each database I learned thereafter (Paciolan, Tessitura, etc.), I would do the same thing—treat it as the basis for everything I would do in the development shop. It helped that I had been a gift processor, so I knew how long it took to enter a batch or run acknowledgment letters. I also knew that I could rely on list pulls and exports or extractions to get me the data I needed to make decisions during my annual giving career. When I worked as a major gift officer, I would create my own queries to help manage my portfolio of donors and update my activities. This ease with the database led me from the major gift side of a multimillion-dollar campaign at a healthcare system foundation to taking their senior director of development operations position and managing their advancement services team. Because I had been in that team's shoes before, I knew how to set realistic expectations with executive leadership for how long requests would take. The foundation's chief development officer (CDO) at the time once asked me which position I preferred—major gifts or advancement services. I said either; I would go wherever the foundation needed me most. I honestly enjoyed both types of positions as well as the management of people to make things successful and efficient, and to accomplish goals.

START WITH A DATA PLAN

Creating a data-driven culture for your team or department starts with the leadership. If you don't make the fundraising database the hull of your ship, your fundraising team will never be able to set sail.

When I speak at conferences about this subject, attendees almost always ask, "What if my data is a mess?" It's okay; you have to start somewhere. Just as you establish an annual giving plan for the year, you need to establish a data plan and time-line for the projects you want to accomplish with the system. Is data visualization a priority for your team? Go backwards. Start with reports you need and then figure out the data that needs to be cleaned first. Establish a month-by-month time-line with goals and objectives. The questions to answer in your data plan can include:

- What is the end result or data project to accomplish?
- What data needs to be cleaned to get to the end result?
- How long will it take to clean the data?
- What staff or contract resources will need to be used?
- What is the anticipated return on investment (ROI) of this project?
- What software enhancements are needed for this project?

Write your data plan down in a Word document or even on a whiteboard, and then use it as a tool for your team and your executive leadership for strategic planning purposes so you can advocate and invest in data-supported technologies for your department.

DATA-DRIVEN LEADERSHIP

It starts at the top. First, a development team leader needs to establish a strong foundation of development operations in your team. Remember that your database is the engine of all your operations, so garbage in is garbage out.

Next, look to enhance data management, processing, research, and portfolio management practices within your team. If you are a team of one, think about things you can do each day or during part of your day to establish these practices.

It is imperative that every fundraising leader educates and focuses their team on data-driven practices. It should be everyone's priority to make the database the center of operations because a data-driven fundraising culture is the future of every nonprofit no matter the size. The large institutions such as hospitals and universities have been implementing these practices for over a decade. It is time for the rest of the nonprofit sector to catch up. As a leader, you must focus gift officers on moves management and the weekly recording of actions in the database. It's also important to reorganize staff roles and department structure based on data-driven decision-making. A leader must hold team members accountable through reporting and weekly updates. And last but certainly not least, make data-driven hiring decisions. Make sure all your job descriptions emphasize the use of data through your team. New team members should be ready to fit into this data-driven culture of updating actions or steps in the database, pulling lists, or creating useful reports.

APPLYING ANALYTICS TO FUNDRAISING

Every year, our employer and global philanthropy firm BWF surveys clients about how analytics had been applied in their shops: 45% were using it to establish financial projections, 49% were setting fundraising goals, 51% were analyzing staff performance, 55% were using analytics in direct mail segmentation, 63% were applying analytics to pipeline and portfolio management, and 81% were using it to identify prospective donors.

The arts sector was traditionally behind the curve in using advanced fundraising analytics practices until Josh and I deployed a pilot project introducing the concept of analytics to arts organizations using the Tessitura database. This project was featured in the 2016 August edition of *The Chronicle of Philanthropy* and is now being used by more than 20 arts and culture institutions around the globe.

What Josh and I found is that arts organizations needed to strategically identify prospects within their own donor, ticket buyer, and subscriber bases. But how? The answer was predictive fundraising models. The organizations would select four models with variables customized to their data. For example, the major gift model would tell an organization the likelihood of a prospect making a major gift with the amount determined by the organization. The planned giving model would indicate the likelihood of a prospect of making a planned gift. Donor or member acquisition models would indicate the likelihood of a ticket buyer converting to a donor or member. The capital campaign model would predict the likelihood of a prospect making a capital campaign gift.

The process begins by applying custom scoring to specific patterns in the organization's data, and every record in your database is rated. Then, predictive modeling follows a defined, tailored, and tested process. To extract the data, a query request form tailored to arts organizations is sent to the organization. When the results are delivered, the models not only help you identify great prospects that may need more attention, but it also show you where you may be wasting your efforts in portfolio management.

One of the biggest obstacles in any analytics project is adoption within your organization. Here are some initial steps for creating an analytics intelligent culture within your organization:

1. Create a data strategic plan for your team.
2. Establish a goal for what you want to accomplish using analytics.
3. Do it!

GETTING STARTED WITH AN ANALYTICS PROJECT OR PROGRAM

How do I use analytics to inform best practices? You have to decide whether you are going to do your analytics project in-house or outsource it. Analytics has moved us from best practices to next practices by finding what "actually" works. With analytics, you can maximize the potential of your database by aligning portfolios and metrics to your constituency potential. And you can improve production of your team by investing in a strategic prospect development program that incorporates analytics.

PORTFOLIO MANAGEMENT

As indicated in the BWF survey just discussed, analytics are commonly used to strategically assign your prospects among officers. First, you have to set up a portfolio management system within your database. Almost all databases come with this kind of capability, whether it is in a proposal or plans tab. This project could be a part of your data plan, even if you are a small shop. Next, you must require that officers track their progress with prospects using the portfolio system. Officers must be held accountable to report on their progress with prospects on a weekly basis. This is commonly executed with weekly reports to development leadership so as to hold officers accountable during revenue meetings to track their progress.

MAJOR GIFT PROSPECT IDENTIFICATION AND CULTIVATION

One of my favorite things to do with analytics is to target a pool of major gift prospects using a major gift model. Once these prospects have been identified, you can verify them and immediately assign them to major gift officers' portfolios. If the prospects are in the top 1% of the model, that means they have a 99% likelihood of giving a major gift once cultivated. The officers can then take the reins with these prospects and start cultivating them. You or your officers can invite them to exclusive events like we did in the arts, which included hard-hat tours of the space, major gift prospect events with key artists, patron/stewardship events of an exclusive rehearsal, VIP intermission experiences, opening night performances, new works workshops, and patron tours.

LIST MANAGEMENT AND REPORTING

Once the predictive models have been loaded in the database, any list in the database can then be pulled and segmented using the models. The most common models used for list segmentation were donor acquisition, leadership annual fund, special events, major gifts, and capital campaign. Development officers in the arts, for example, could focus their cultivation efforts on those patrons who attended a particular performance or event by filtering attendees with high major gift model scores and running them through a Patron Activity Report in Tessitura.

DIRECT MAIL SEGMENTATION

Direct mail appeals now have a much better ROI because of analytics. I find that many times annual fund teams (or leaders who previously were in annual fund positions) are the first to adopt analytics due to the nature of their jobs. They are used to dealing with data and are able to beautifully balance the art and science of fundraising. As with all direct mail appeals, you must first create a compelling message, whether it be about education and community efforts, new works initiatives, production activities, hurricane relief, and so forth. Then, I find it's key to build momentum through multichannel messaging, and if at all possible, use a board challenge/matching grant with a deadline to create a sense of urgency. Finally, it's important to use enhanced list segmentation and data analytics. I found the combination of a donor acquisition model + previous giving + top performing zip codes created a great ROI for direct mail appeals at a previous organization.

OVERALL RESULTS
OF PREDICTIVE MODELING

Of course, the whole point of all this data-driven fundraising is to increase revenue. Imagine your customer relationship management (CRM) or database as a fancy Cadillac with all the bells and whistles, but you have yet to learn how to start the car and drive it around the block. Likewise, there is no reason to invest in the fancy analytics tools if the "Cadillac" never leaves the driveway. Analytics is a powerful tool but only as useful as the teams that adopt them into practice. Because I used analytics at previous organizations, I saw substantially increased revenue from individual giving. One arts organization received $20,000 in current use gifts after using their planned giving model for a direct mailing. Another organization raised $100,000 in increased revenue using models in a six-month period. Of equal importance was the hours of time saved by prospect research and development staff in identifying prospective donors. Finally, analytics resulted in the effective portfolio management of prospects among gift officers, so that better decisions could be made on which prospects each officer should approach.

Due to limited time as a director of development, I didn't want to meet with a prospect unless I knew there was a 90% or more chance that they would give the gift I was asking them to give. That's what analytics does—it allows you to make the best strategic decisions with limited time and resources.

CHAPTER DISCUSSION GUIDE

- In an ideal world, without staff, time, or budget constraints, how might you implement analytics at your organization?
- What database project can you create a strategic data plan for your department/team this year?
- How might you implement data visualization (dashboards, infographics, visual impactful reports) in your fundraising shop?
- What steps can you take to adopt a data-driven culture in your team?

2

THE INNOVATIVE FACTOR

Good artists borrow, great artists steal.

—Pablo Picasso

I have a love-hate relationship with *best practices*.

When you are learning something completely new, like waterskiing, you start with the fundamentals. You are told to lean back in the water with the rope between your skis. Your guide tells you to avoid locking your knees. When you first get up on the water, you are focused on staying up. It might not be much fun at first, but you manage to get up and glide behind the boat. This is how I think of "best practices."

After you've waterskied a few times, the fundamentals become instinct and you play a bit. Perhaps you can get started off the dock or begin to slalom, even drop a ski to go on one foot. In other words, you are beginning to have some fun, becoming a better skier, and creating something new. This is "next practices."

A better example is learning a musical instrument. Many children despise practicing the piano. Most will drop out of lessons by middle school. If you ask these same kids as adults about their early piano lessons, they will say they wished they'd stuck with it. When you are learning, you don't sound like Rachmaninoff or Billy Joel. Aunt Rhody's gray goose is probably dead from your playing!

But after years of studying the piano, it begins to click. You just seem to get how the chords line up with melodies, and you begin to improvise. You begin creating something new. It's probably a lot more fun.

So why the love-hate relationship? Surely fundamentals are a good thing, aren't they?

There is a fine line between best practices and conformity. Mastery arrives after the fundamentals are behind us. But if we continue to use the fundamentals as our measure, will we ever drop the ski or jam with a jazz combo? We should be in constant pursuit of the next practices.

Where this plays out is in benchmarking. Surely, a career consultant like me would never say anything bad about benchmarking! Why risk a common revenue stream for professional services? Yes, I will go there. Benchmarking is full of biases and risks, the most common being selection bias, confirmation bias, and unintended consequences.

Let's say your organization needs to raise more money from your major gift officers. You are not sure why other similar institutions raise so much money. Perhaps you need to reconfigure your prospect management metrics. If we can just get each officer to get out there more, we will raise more money.

So you start by conducting or commissioning a benchmarking study for best practices in prospect management.

When you frame the benchmarking study, you talk with the consultant about questions to answer and your peer group. You include a few organizations you admire or that continue to out fundraise your group. The questions include what they track, whether they use a weighted score card or incentives, and so on. The consultant's analyst team begins to make calls or send a digital survey. They compile the results into visuals and present a report. You review the findings and realize your aspirant peers do some things differently than you do. So, you adapt your organization's prospect management system to more closely align with these organizations. Was that a wise move?

There are some significant unknowns in this scenario. You selected the peer group based on your experience. Are these organizations truly representative? This is selection bias. You determined the reason these aspirant peers raised more money than you was because of their prospect management system. Do you really know that the prospect management differences are the source of their advantage over you? Perhaps they are located in a wealthier or more philanthropic community. Or they may have less philanthropic competition or situationally urgent priorities for their community. Your decision to emulate their prospect management system is confirmation bias.

Perhaps your prospect management system was optimal for your organization already. Perhaps the reason your team was not raising as much money was inaccessible program staff or uninspiring priorities. There might be danger in focusing change management energy on the wrong problem.

In your pursuit of best practices, you may have entered into a zone of unintended consequences. How do you really know?

BEGINNINGS OF INNOVATION

This is where innovation begins. Once you escape the trap of conformity, you begin to look ahead for new ways to be better or to improve your organization. To take our music analogy further, you already know the chords, it's time to improvise and have some fun.

How might an innovative fundraiser tackle the same question prompting the benchmarking study?

The organization needs to raise more money from its major gift officers. You could start by assembling lots of potential factors such as prospect management activity, case for support, constituent wealth, portfolio composition, organizational culture, team motivation, officer tenure, distractions, team skills, access to program staff or researchers, CEO involvement, volunteer involvement, organizational reputation, staff esteem, supporting infrastructure, and so on.

Next, you might begin doing some controlled studies (using your analysts or a consultant) within your ecosystem. For example, using equally sized samples of donors who said *yes* and prospects who said no, you ask why they gave and listen for the differences. Rather than describing the successful gift approaches, you are discovering the characteristics distinguishing between successful and unsuccessful approaches. You may also conduct some relationship modeling of your fundraisers. Split them by production or yield and survey them all with the same questions about culture, motivation, headwinds, and so forth. Look at how the two groups answer differently. Analyze the differences in activity metrics. You are beginning to understand not which practices are *best*, but which practices are *best for you*.

The pursuit of next practices flows out of mastery of the fundamentals. It also flows out of passion for improvement. My friend Kate Chamberlain of Memorial Sloan Kettering introduced me to the Toyota Kata principles popular in the Lean Six Sigma world. I would have never thought to apply continuous process improvement concepts from manufacturing to fundraising, but she did. And it made total sense.

A key principle in Toyota Kata is to understand where you want to be—or your *target condition*. In the previous example, your target condition is raising X money from your major gift team. In a series of sequential incremental tests, you try one simple change and evaluate. Perhaps you start with a digital warming piece immediately before discovery calls. Did call acceptance improve? Now, what is the next one thing you can do? It is a never-ending, or *continuous*, pursuit of improving your process.

Maybe the Kata approach is not right for you. But this is an example of an innovator deciding in her own environment to pursue next practices.

I get it. There is safety in the box. Thinking outside of it can be scary. As Bilbo Baggins said, "It's a dangerous business, Frodo, going out your door. You step onto the road, and if you don't keep your feet, there's no knowing where you might be swept off to."

Regardless of the warning, Bilbo went out that door and became the most revered Hobbit ever—that is until his nephew Frodo decided to take the same risk.

WALKING OUT THE DOOR

Being innovative is a choice; it is not an innate personality trait. What holds us back is fear. What we fear the most are risks to our professional self-preservation. Usually, this fear is irrational.

Over my career, I've worked with hundreds of nonprofits. A few of my clients raise over $1 billion annually. A few have raised less than $10 million. Most are somewhere in between. I've seen innovators at all levels. I've yet to come across a development professional moved out because they were too innovative. If they were moved out of an organization, it was usually because of interpersonal conflicts, inflexibility, or failures to communicate. They had to win. Innovation is about trying. It is not about winning.

We are in a period of a substantial talent gap in fundraising. There are many more positions than there are fundraisers to fill them. It is an employee's market. This is the best time to walk out that door in the Bilbo Baggins sense. It is time to try new things to make your organization better, to make the industry better, and to make you better.

Here are some tips from one innovator to another.

THERE IS POWER IN COFFEE

Winning over others to your new ideas is rarely about excellent debate skills. Making friends in your organization is so much more effective. I'm not saying you must consume caffeine to make friends. But do get out there and connect socially with your colleagues. If you are working to live, you are not really living. There are opportunities to connect with so many amazing people all around you.

Mark Horstman of Manager Tools once said that there are three ways to persuade others. The first way is through the exertion of your role. A parent can persuade a child to do what is asked because of the parent-child role differential. Similarly, employees will do what the boss says. The second way is through the exertion of your expertise. You might try what a consultant like me suggests because you think I may be more of an expert in the area of interest. Perhaps you reach out to a researcher or professor for advice. If you follow their advice, it is not because you must do so. Rather, you decide to do so because you acknowledge their expertise. The third way is through the exertion of your relationship. If you ask your friend to help you move your couch, they will likely help you if they are able. You are not in a position over your friend. Your friend is unlikely to desire your expertise in couch relocation. Instead, they help because you would do the same for them. A relationship has a quid pro quo of mutual bond development.

If you have a new area of innovation you are trying to implement, all three of these persuasion techniques are at your disposal. If you are the boss, you can ask your employees to follow your instructions. They will do so because of the employer-employee contract. If you are the more experienced fundraiser, you may ask your peers to follow your lead. They may do so if they acknowledge the differences in your respective skills. But the most effective way to make change is to ask friends to go along with you.

PRACTICE INNOVATION

Legos were among my favorite childhood toys. Their popularity continues to this day. Most sets of Legos have all the pieces to build one specific vehicle, building, or scene. They include instructions for assembling each block into the image on the box. Most kids (and some adults) build the item on the box initially. Over time, the item is disassembled and the Legos join a communal bin. And a few stragglers remain on the floor to punish the unexpecting parents' feet as they walk barefoot across the carpet.

With Legos, you are presented with the opportunity to explore both best practices and next practices. Personally, I found creating something new from the bin of Legos to be much more fun than following the instructions. But by building multiple sets, I learned about structural soundness, assembling wheels and axels, and when it makes sense to use which block in context of the whole. This playing became practice for innovation. My new creation was all mine. The more I built new things, the more creative and successful I became.

Innovation flows out of mastery. Mastery flows out of practice. Before you begin to try the new thing for your organization, it is imperative to practice the fundamentals. Then, the fundamentals become building blocks of innovation. As you begin to innovate, you will fail more often than you succeed. But this practice helps you refine your skills as an innovator.

Forgiving Cultures Foster Innovation

Later in the book we will unpack qualities of a great leader. In that chapter, I will describe some of the research into character conducted by the renowned executive coach Fred Kiel. In his research for the book *Return on Character*, he presented the correlation between forgiving leaders and innovation. Leaders who are forgiving of themselves and others have the most innovative workforces.

If you are a fundraising leader or manager, ask yourself if there is room for innovation in your organization. Will you be punitive if your employee fails? If you are a practitioner yourself, will you forgive yourself if you fail? Failing is critical for improvement. Are you able to celebrate the ambition for organizational improvement over the lack of success? If you are not, you may never get that innovative improvement you so desire.

Pursue Other Innovators

The education sector has among the most effective professional associations in the philanthropic sector. CASE, the Council for Advancement and Support of Education, convenes learning opportunities and fosters research to benefit educational fundraisers. For years, the joke has been that CASE really stands for "Copy And Steal Everything." However, I would suggest you consider copying and stealing a little bit more to be a great innovator.

Now, similar to my cautions around biases in benchmarking, there is great risk in copying specifics. Nevertheless, get out there in your industry and copy the ambition, aspirations, and resilient pursuits of great innovators. I am a better innovator because I've learned from so many innovators who went before me. This continues to be my pursuit. I am a member of the Giving Institute, which is an assortment of the greatest service firms in our sector, because we make each other better. We may compete for business, but we are all trying to advance nonprofits. If I closed myself off from them, I would not only limit my own innovation, I would do a disservice to the countless worthy charities benefiting from our shared knowledge.

Go and visit other nonprofits. Find the people writing blogs or speaking at conferences. Get to know them and find out what drives them. When innovators are part of your ecosystem, you will become more innovative yourself.

EMBRACE WORTHINESS OF MISSION

In watching a recent interview with Seth Godin, I was struck by his description of sales. Roughly, he said if we have something that will provide others with value or satisfaction, we have the responsibility to share it. Sales is not persuading someone do something they do not want to do. Rather, it is letting them into the opportunity to do something that they would really like to do.

Believing in the value you offer, and that your organization provides, is the fuel in your innovation tank. If you are working in a nonprofit, I would suspect you do so because you care about something more than maximizing shareholder value. Nonprofits exist only to help. By their nature, they are, or should be, selfless. Whether it is protecting the environment or feeding children, educating the population or finding cures, nonprofits offer something both recipients and donors deeply desire.

Is your mission worth your efforts to pursue next practices? Why are you there? If the cause is urgent and right, you have no excuse but to put the best you have to offer into your organization.

THERE ISN'T ENOUGH TIME

I have a friend who is a stay-at-home parent. His wife works outside the home; he manages the home front. As we all know, there is always something to do at home. There are always dishes to wash, rooms to clean, items to fix, yardwork to do, bills to pay, and lunches to make. He realized that when his spouse came home from work, he would continue to do housework rather than spend quality time with his spouse. They were married because they liked each other's company and wanted to spend a life together. But his focus was pulled away by daily distractions. His solution was to set work hours for himself. After 7:00 p.m. each night, he decided everything else can wait until morning. If all the dishes weren't washed, they would still be there during his housework hours. He said it was the best thing he ever did, and their relationship improved.

About a decade ago, companies began implementing FedEx Days. These immersion events protected time periodically for organization-wide innovation. Employees pursued, researched, baked, and tested new ideas. By the next morning, they presented these ideas to the company. The name "FedEx Day" emerged from the need to deliver overnight, just like the logistics company. Innovation was scheduled. Because it was scheduled, it was practiced. Because it was practiced, innovation flourished.

I like to say that *time management* is really a misnomer. It might be more accurately called *guilt management*. There is no time, only guilt around what I failed to do. Ultimately, what we choose to do is a statement about what we value. If self-preservation is what we value, we will invest time in compliance with the norms. If self-advancement is what we value, we will invest time in self. If organizational advancement is what we value, we will invest time in innovation. Do your values align to your desired time management? If not, how might you make the change? If not, what might you do to bring that alignment into focus?

CHALLENGE CONFORMITY

I encourage you to push through the safety of best practices and begin to improvise. Walk out that front door and go on an adventure. Although you might find some dragons to slay, you might also find a magic ring. You will definitely have stories to tell, and you will be better for it.

Try one new thing. Explore one new idea. Go have coffee with like-minded colleagues. Practice creation. Be willing to fail. Be willing to let your colleagues fail. Find industry mentors and friends. Devote time to what could be, not just to what is. Your organization is worth it. *You* are worth it.

~~~

REASON TO INNOVATE

Let's have an honest conversation with ourselves about why we innovate as fundraisers. We innovate for others, for the team, and for the industry, but we also innovate for ourselves. We innovate for the challenge, to solve a problem, or reach a revenue goal. We innovate for the exciting opportunity to create and be part of something bigger. We innovate to find creative ways to help increase efficiencies, to find new ways to increase revenue, and to adapt to our surroundings.

We innovate to advance knowledge in our field and industry, maybe even leave a legacy. We innovate to help others advance their shops too, so our nonprofits can survive in this ever-changing philanthropic landscape. Innovation can be scary; it takes risk, guts, and persistence. You might encounter critics and pessimists, but you must persist and continue to innovate.

YOU TOO CAN BE AN INNOVATOR

We as fundraisers might have a tendency to acquiesce our own creativity to our colleagues and assume it is only reserved for creative professions such as artistic directors, creative directors, graphic designers, marketing and communications teams, and event producers. But creativity belongs to the fundraiser. Go to any special event or major gift cultivation. The art of fundraising is prevalent. But why stop there? Why reserve our fundraising art and creativity for only certain parts of fundraising? Why don't we harness innovation in all aspects of our field?

CONNECTING THE DOTS

Innovation is about connecting the dots. We use our knowledge and experiences to connect the dots in a creative and brave way. Who knows better about connecting the dots than us fundraisers? We as fundraisers are primed and groomed for innovation! Most of us by nature are networking addicts, always trying to find the common ground to relate to our colleagues and donors. So why don't we also use our connective energy to bring together ideas to create the next fundraising practices? Is it fear? Is it self-doubt? Is it time?

Perhaps starting my fundraising career more than 20 years ago in Silicon Valley changed my perception of innovation. In addition to learning about terrific wine, I was constantly surrounded by new technologies, ideas, and innovations. I remember passing creative online dating billboards on the highway and friends getting this cool new device that recorded TV for the first time. This endless inertia of innovation was exciting to live around. Silicon Valley continues to serve as an incubator for innovation that now other large cities strive to replicate. I was working for a theater company in Silicon Valley when I realized the people I met, like Jim who invented this tech device, or Jeff who created that start-up, or Ann in the C-suite of that famous tech company, were just people—people who dared to dream, connected the dots, and endeavored to be creative within their own areas of expertise. I was able to demystify the innovator and realize they were people just like me. I think the moment I began to break down the ingredients of a brilliant idea or concept into the sum of its parts, I was able to take the mystery out of innovation and realize my own ability to innovate.

DISSECTING THE GENIUS

Anyone who knows me knows I am a huge musical theater fan, so let's dissect the musical *Hamilton* by the genius Lin-Manuel Miranda, for example. What makes *Hamilton* so brilliant is the convergence of several existing concepts and connections. In interviews, Lin speaks about reading Ron Chernow's 2004 biography about Alexander Hamilton on a beach while on vacation. In Lin's mind, he jumped to the conclusion that this book needed to be a musical; he could see the musical take shape in his mind. In the theater community, Lin was already known for creating the hip-hop show *Bring It On: The Musical* and the acclaimed *In the Heights*, but prior to 2008, few outside of the theater knew about these shows until *In the Heights* won 2008 Tony Awards for best musical, original score, and choreography. In his earlier musicals, Lin connected the dots between two existing concepts: the music genre of hip-hop and freestyle rap along with the performing art form of musicals. Lin was before his time with these musicals, but he saw the dots and had the guts to connect them and make them something so much greater. Add the ingredient of time as he developed his next masterpiece of *Hamilton* based on an existing storyline. Now, he has overlaid his previous innovation (of hip-hop, jazz, R&B, and the Broadway musical) with a good story that needs to be told in modern context. Bring in your trusted Broadway friends and collaborators: music director, choreographer, director, and producers, and you have a smash hit. Then, thanks to social media and word of mouth, you create a worldwide phenomenon. But it all had to do with the right concept, the right people, and the right timing.

INNOVATIVE ADVANCEMENT PRACTICES

It's 2001 and Josh Birkholz dissects the FICO credit score. He makes the connection that if the credit-score model can be used to determine whether someone has a likelihood of receiving a good line of credit, then turning the model upside down could determine a donor's likelihood of making a major gift. Thus, by connecting a dot that existed, analyzing it, and literally turning it upside down, Josh was able to create a new invention of predictive fundraising models for our sector. Josh then wrote about it in 2008, penning the book

Fundraising Analytics: Using Data to Guide Strategy. By introducing analytics to the nonprofit fundraising sector, Josh changed the science of fundraising and how we as fundraisers do business.

Fast forward to 2013, I meet Josh while overseeing development operations for a hospital system foundation. I worked with Josh and his colleagues to implement four predictive models for the foundation team. The following year, I leave the hospital system to return to my passion—the performing arts. The managing director of a regional theater and the director of development tasked me with bringing the best practices of fundraising I had learned at the hospital to the theater. After one month of learning a new database, Tessitura, I found an automation feature in the database that seemed perfectly suited for Josh's models. By connecting the dots and importing these fundraising models into the automated feature in Tessitura, Josh and I were able to introduce cutting-edge analytics to the arts.

I have always been prone to innovation within a database. Previously, I had created a custom fund balance reporting system for more than 200 endowment and restricted funds within the Raiser's Edge. I remember sitting in a Blackbaud forum of development operations professionals across the city and asking if anyone had created and adapted this kind of fund balance report in the database before. I guess I had stumped the audience, because literally no one acknowledged my question—they simply moved on to the next one. I felt defeated. Perhaps my complex fund balance report would not work in this system? A friend approached me after the session and recalled having a similar endowment fund report when she worked for a hospital system. This small seed of encouragement made me realize that I knew it could be done. I was inspired to collaborate with a local database consultant (saving tens of thousands of dollars investing in other financial reporting software) to create this custom reporting system using Crystal reports and the database. Through months of data cleanup and implementation, we were finally able to accomplish this automated reporting system. As a result, the reports were no longer run by hand in Excel over a two-week period (and using a macro created by a former employee's husband). Now, data was imported into the system and reports were run and distributed in two to three days. This project was truly a marriage between efficiency and innovation. Another project I worked on in which innovation played a role was using a rebate company and software import tool to quickly assist with gift entry for a massive employee campaign, but that is a story for another time. The point is that I constantly wanted to make processes better and more efficient. I wanted to challenge myself, in part so as not to get bored, and to maximize the database system in the process.

FAILING WELL

Innovation is far beyond a buzzword now. Today, innovation is more than a concept; it's a culture and an economy. At one large tech company, they created an adaptive culture for innovation, a flat structure in which an innovative idea can come from any employee and be heard. They also know how to "fail well." This company is known to throw parties on their campus for projects that needed to die. They celebrate the innovation, but also the opportunity to spend their resources in other more productive ideas.

We must combat our fear of failure as fundraisers. We must persist past previous failed attempts and own up to the failures for what they were, and then let them go. Whether it was missing a revenue goal, losing a valued employee, completing an analytics project with little to no findings, or pursuing a fundraising idea that never took off, you must try and then try again. None of us are perfect, but it is persistence that will eventually pay off.

TIMELINE OF INNOVATION

Innovation does involve being in the right place, with the right people, at the right time. However, if you are constantly thinking toward innovative practices and the next great idea for our industry, your probability of finding that idea at the right time is significantly higher than not cultivating innovation at all. A friend of mine once worked for a hard-drive manufacturer in Silicon Valley and told me at the time that most tech companies based their fiscal year planning and budgeting on the quarter instead of the year. Therefore, tech companies were planning four times ahead of the typical company, constantly adapting and innovating to keep ahead of the curve. We need to think about fundraising innovation with this same kind of speed and sense of urgency.

When I was a part of the analytics pilot project for Tessitura, I set a six-month timeframe for myself. During those six months I would implement the models, see how much money I was able to raise using them, and then speak at a Tessitura conference session in Florida about the experience. My colleagues and I implemented the predictive models in December, and then over the next six months used them as much as possible within individual giving for prospecting, portfolio management, list pulls, reporting, major-gift cultivation, and donor acquisition mailings. As a result, my team and I saved hours of time in prospecting and research, and we raised $100K more using these models than was raised six months prior. The following year, we went on to raise $1 million more using and implementing predictive fundraising models in every aspect of our annual fund along with other next fundraising practices. It is important to set a goal for developing and implementing an innovative project that you would like to accomplish and create month-by-month benchmarks toward that deadline.

SPACES FOR INNOVATION

Innovation and creativity must happen in a safe space, giving the innovator time to think and adapt. This was particularly true for the first theater I worked for that hosted new musical workshops and writers retreats for Broadway composers, writers, and lyricists. These creative teams were taking new or existing content and transforming them into new musicals but needed a safe and quiet space to do so. What this theater company did was give them the time and resources to write and create.

Similarly, in my hometown of Houston, an "Innovation District" has been created by a cooperative with various business and city entities, universities, hospitals, and nonprofits. Spanning from downtown to the medical center, this district started housing incubator projects. Regional cities are creating these areas or spaces for innovation because they know innovation means investing in our future local and global economy. Businesses want to quickly import ideas and funding into their own cities instead of exporting them to other cities or countries. The innovative economy is beginning to thrive and weave into the fabric of our cities, but it takes thinking, convening, and community building to build a robust innovative economy within a city. At global consulting firms like Accenture, "innovation hubs" exist where clients bring forth ideas for implementation. What are we doing as fundraisers to join this innovation movement to advance our own profession? How are we in our Association of Fundraising Professionals (AFP), Association of Professional Researchers for Advancement (Apra), Association for Healthcare Philanthropy (AHP), or CASE conferences creating and sparking each other toward fundraising innovation? Whether we find physical or virtual spaces to convene, innovation and creativity are vital to the advancement of our profession.

Catalysts for Creativity

How do we cultivate creativity within ourselves and others? To become a vessel for innovation, it first takes practice in creative thought, risk taking, and collaboration. As innovators, we thrive on others' innovations. We celebrate one another's successes. We are passionate about talking about the innovation, encouraging one another toward the next best idea and project. I would not be the innovator I am today without Josh's encouragement and support. He is a colleague who leads with humility and pushes me and others toward innovative greatness. When others propel you to think higher of yourself, you become a better version of yourself and inspire others to do the same. You not only pay it forward to those who invested in you in the first place, but you also inspire others to do the same for their benefit and that of our industry. If we can inspire greatness among one another, then the creativity will happen. It does not take much to be a change agent for yourself or for your peers, but it does take humility. Once you are excited about your innovation, others will follow and get excited too. You then get excited about their innovations and start telling others about how innovative they are as well. By encouraging each other's innovations, we become catalysts for one another's creativity.

COLLABORATION CREATES INNOVATION

As the adage goes, "a rising tide lifts all boats," and that is how collaboration lifts innovation. Innovation can happen anywhere and with anyone who is willing to participate, if you and they are open to it. The key is to surround yourself with like-minded innovators who want to change the nonprofit sector just as you do. It doesn't take the smartest person in the room or one with an advanced degree, but it does take the most creative, most daring person who is willing to take action on their ideas.

We must surround ourselves with positive, encouraging, and motivating people who inspire us toward creativity. How might we create a culture in our fundraising field to think outside the box? We, as development professionals, must adopt for-profit innovation strategies, structures, and practices of cultivating creativity among our employees and peers. We have to throw out the words "we have always done it this way." We have to assume there is always a better way. It is the only way we as nonprofits will stay ahead of the curve and be able to adapt to the changing philanthropic landscape.

THOUGHT LEADERSHIP

After cultivating creativity and inspiring innovation in others—whether through conferences or virtual webinars—it is then that we become thought leaders and resources for our industry. You will have to put yourself out there at first to gain credibility. But once you notice that first spark at a conference session about your innovative idea, peers and colleagues start to take notice and stay in touch. Then word starts to spread, and more colleagues begin to take notice. This is because you make intentional steps to surround yourself with a network of those who believe in you and your ability to innovate. You are also able to write frequently and talk passionately about your innovation, persuading others to take part in it. Thought leadership does not happen overnight, but it is intentional, strategic, and thoughtful. Thought leadership means taking the time to write a blog post or collaborate on a case study about innovative practices. As you surround yourself with other creative catalysts who help spark and flame your creativity—whether it is a consultant, peer, manager, or nonprofit leader—when you succeed, we all succeed as a result.

In conclusion, GO! Go after the next big fundraising idea—find it, take it, mold it, and shape it like potter's clay. Build a creation of your own and put your own unique and creative stamp on it. Create something to inspire and motivate colleagues to innovate and inform the next best practices in our industry. Then share your new idea with everyone you know and see what happens.

Chapter Discussion Guide

- What ways might you spur yourself or others toward being "catalysts of creativity"?
- What fundraising idea could you take and mold and steal into a new idea?
- On a scale of 1 to 10 (with 10 being the highest), how would you rate the innovative nature of your development team? What ideas do you have for increasing your team's score?
- What are three ways you can help cultivate a culture of innovation within your organization?
- Name some conventions or group meetings that already exist that can be cultivated into creative hubs for innovation.
- What keeps you from using your connective energy to bring together ideas to create the next practices in fundraising? Fear? Self-doubt? Time? Resources?
- How might we set up ourselves and our teams for success or for "failing well"?

3

THE
COLLABORATIVE
FACTOR

For too long, we nonprofits have been siloed from one another.
While all of us do different things and play different roles, there is
one thing that binds all of us together: Community.

—Vu Le

In 2015, the American Marketing Association published a
paper by a cross-university team of researchers called
"Developing Donor Relationships: The Role of the Breadth
of Giving." Although the findings of this study may not seem
groundbreaking, it foreshadowed a substantial headwind in
fundraising organizations.

The key conclusion of the study was that "improvements
in donation variety increase the likelihood that the donor

will make a subsequent donation, increase the donation amount, and reduce the sensitivity of donations to negative macroeconomic shocks." In other words, when donors give to multiple areas of an organization, they will likely give again, they will give more, and they will be more resilient (Farnoosh Khodakarami, J. Andrew Petersen, and Rajkumar Venkatesan, "Developing Donor Relationships: The Role of the Breadth of Giving," *Journal of Marketing*, 79, no. 4 (2015)).

Since reading this study several years ago, I had my team of analysts dive into the same topic for many of our firm's clients. We studied the effect not only of multiple designations, but also multiple approaches. We analyzed prospects pursued only by one major gift officer. We compared these to prospects pursued by fundraisers from different areas of the organizations (different college of the university, different service area in healthcare, etc.). Our findings corroborated all of the researchers' points. Not only did the donors give more overall when compared to single-pursuit donors, they gave more to the first area of interest.

COLLABORATION BETWEEN FUNDRAISERS

Single cases notwithstanding, the research suggests donors prefer multiple touchpoints within an organization, that they are less sensitive to "toe-stepping" than generally believed, and that they give more when approached by multiple fundraisers. So protecting one's turf really has no place in fundraising. Where did this competitive portfolio protectionism originate? In my opinion, these walls are unintended consequences of poorly designed prospect management strategies and leadership deficiencies.

In the past, and perhaps still in the present for less sophisticated organizations, very little activity data was entered into the database system. The advancement services professionals focused their efforts on gift administration and high-level reports. Fundraisers were evaluated by how much money they raised. Because little data existed, about all that was available was portfolio assignment and total giving. This was an easy breakdown for a simple report. If a donor was assigned to a fundraiser and that donor gave, the fundraiser would get credit. Fundraiser job security was tied to the production of their portfolio.

This system is very easy to game. If your self-preservation is tied to portfolio performance, you can either work really hard to raise more money from your portfolio or you can assemble a portfolio of people already giving despite your efforts. As long as you protect your turf, your job is secure.

Over the years, this turf protection culture took hold. Now, most organizations can calculate the actual officer effect on giving. Prospect researchers identify prospects with capacity. Officers can meet, cultivate, and solicit gifts. But many organizations have held tight to the portfolio dollars metric. Rather than portfolios being comprised of the prospects officers intend to solicit in a defined time period, they remain an assortment of the top donors to the officers' respective areas.

In this environment, there is no incentive to share prospects. Evidence of protecting this cultural dogma range from officers saying to each other, "We have to protect our donors from toe-stepping. These donors can't be approached from all sides," to pushing back on high-capacity prospects because they are not already giving. Fundraising is a profession of motivating others to give, not maintaining relationships of donors already giving. Donor experience management is the responsibility of donor relations. Cultivating and asking is the responsibility of fundraising. In other words, fundraisers are the sales team, not customer service. Leadership can counter this headwind by focusing the metrics on what people have control over in the relationship. And collaboration should be celebrated, not discouraged.

I purchased my first iPod not long after they emerged on the market. Later, when the iPhone came out, I was an early adopter. Later still, my wife and daughters each got their own iPhones. We became part of the iTunes ecosystem. We bought Mac computers for our home. My daughters bought Mac laptops for school. I bought an iPad for my music scores so I could turn pages with a foot pedal when performing. After going to the Apple Store many times, an Apple salesperson realized I was a business owner. He reached out to me about considering becoming a Mac office. My value with Apple was deepening because of the breadth of my experience. If I had been held in a proverbial portfolio of the initial iPod group, my value would have been limited.

Donor value increases from the breadth of experience with an organization. Collaboration, not only within the early stages of the journey but at the major gift officer level, benefits the donor and deepens the relationship.

A modern fundraiser is in the business of empowering philanthropy. If personal preservation gets in the way of empowerment, you do a disservice to the donor and to your organization. If the metrics system discourages collaboration, your organization does the same disservice. From my experience, rogue collaborators, even in these environments, rarely suffer from their donor-centeredness. Most often, they are the fundraisers who climb the organizational chart.

Collaboration with Other Development Professionals

The collaboration I'm talking about is not only among fundraisers, but also with the supporting infrastructure of your development program. In a study my team conducted for a major research university, we found that top-performing fundraisers, defined as the 20% raising 80% of the dollars, actually met with the prospect development team and donor relations team twice as often as the other 80%.

Big consulting and law firms have a concept called "lowest-cost biller." Essentially, if another employee can do the same task effectively at a lower cost or at a greater scale, they should do so. If another biller could do the task much better for the same cost, they should do it. In our current economy, it is very difficult to hire people willing to sit down with donors and ask them for money. Because of the staffing shortage, we are seeing increased transiency and wage inflation. Fundraisers are the highest-cost billers in the development organization.

By contrast, it is not as difficult to hire people to manage the donor experience, identify prospects, track activity, to enter gifts, to write reports. If fundraisers are completing tasks that could be done as effectively by others in the organization at a lower cost or a greater scale, this work should be off-loaded to them.

Although structurally the lowest-cost biller concept works in fundraising, few executives are able to make the cost-benefit case for the back office staff. It is easy to connect total dollars raised to the number of fundraisers. But few have the data at their fingertips to describe the benefits of increased time devoted to fundraising.

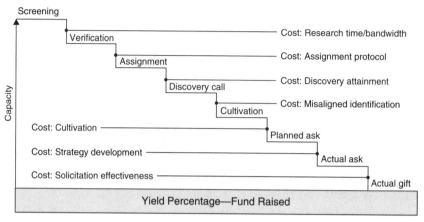

FIGURE 3.1   Pipeline Yield Analysis
Source: Josh Birkholz, BWF 2019.

My preferred method for making this case is to borrow a concept from capacity analysis. As described in Chapter 1, The Data-Driven Factor, overall file capacity is compared to organizational yield or "share of wallet." If an organization raises 5% of the file capacity in the campaign, what happened to the other 95%. Is the final yield completely in the hands of the frontline fundraisers?

As shown in Figure 3.1, the bottom bar is the final yield against file capacity. After screening the database, there is a total capacity number. It should be pointed out that all wealth is not publicly available and not all records match to screening. Nonetheless, this is a good starting denominator for yield analysis. Following the screening and likely predictive modeling or other scoring, the prospect research team verifies the names. This quick vetting process is a risk- management step, much as underwriting is for lending, to determine if the prospect is valid. Not all names can be verified. Not all verified names are deemed prospects. This is likely the greatest drop from file capacity on the journey to ultimate yield.

After verification, some portion of the names do make their way to the assignment process. Depending on portfolio sizes, officer biases, or staff capacity, many viable names do not get assigned. This is the next drop on the way to final yield numbers.

Assigned names then move into a discovery process. This is the first step of reaching out personally to the prospect to meet. Often the calls are a bit cold even if the relationship with the organization is warm. To date, their giving has been in response to organizational cultivation and not individual cultivation. This transition is not comfortable for everyone. For most fundraisers, these first interactions are the least favorite part of their jobs. Four out of every five clients I work with have issues with discovery volume. It is not uncommon to find that fewer than 20% of assigned names are ever contacted. This is the first drop in yield attributable to the frontline.

When the discovery call actually takes place, sometimes the fundraiser determines the name is not a viable prospect. This information is important to share back to the prospect development team so they can calibrate their identification criteria. This misaligned identification is the next cost against capacity.

When the cultivation process begins, officers will enter strategy notes including the anticipated future ask level. Although about 20% of fundraisers, and typically the more successful ones, enter ask levels consistent with capacity, the average ask level from our research is 44% of capacity. Some drop in yield is attributable to the boldness of the officer. When the actual ask happens, occasionally this is less than intended. The final gifted amount may be lower or none at all.

Unsuccessful asks are the final draw. What is left is the ultimate yield used in analysis.

Every one of these points are opportunities for collaboration and improving organizational yield. Verification can be improved by devoting resources to researchers or collaborating with outside service providers. Leadership can set purposeful assignment protocols by encouraging regular portfolio churn. Digital marketing can provide warming and initial interactions to ease the transition from organizational to individual cultivation. Officers can maintain a feedback loop with prospect development and analytics about successful and unsuccessful discovery interactions. Experienced fundraisers can mentor new fundraisers about solicitation level setting, and so forth. Improving each of these stages can result in measurable, increased return on investment for the program. For example, a 20% increase in discovery attainment could mean a 1–2% increase in campaign yield.

EMBRACE INCLUSIVITY

Because it is the 21st century, I would hope that your organization is making every effort to build a diverse workforce worthy of the constituency it represents. Surely the benefits of diversity are multiple in providing true donor-centeredness, being a responsible employer, expanding perspectives, exposing blind spots, and being a much more exciting place to work. The benefits of diversity can only be realized with committed inclusivity.

In addition to racial diversity and personal expression identities, remember you also have diversity of roles, career stage, age, experience, and personality. *True collaboration values every voice.*

It may be a cliché to use a sports analogy in this type of book, and perhaps the analogy is too commonplace, but American football is a great example of inclusivity. Each role on the field is absolutely necessary for the success of the entire team. The lineman protects the quarterback and makes room for the running backs to run. The receivers can only catch a pass thrown to them. Very few people can handle the stress of a placekicker in key moments of the game. Although different roles may have different economics behind them, each person is valued.

In an organization, roles and hierarchies are necessary to scale a business and meet donor needs. But no one person is better than another. The gift administration team is managing the funds so you can be with donors. Donor relations is keeping in touch with your donors so you can pursue new prospects. Admins are there for your time management. To be a collaborative fundraiser is to value everyone around you.

COLLABORATION WITH VOLUNTEERS

I am amazed at how many people do this work free of charge. Some of the most successful fundraisers I have ever met are board members and other volunteers. Their personal commitment and contagious passion energize me every time I speak at a board meeting or meet with a volunteer individually. If professional fundraisers are constantly honing their skills, why are some volunteers so darn successful? We will dive into the why they succeed in Chapter 4. For now, let's focus on collaborating with the volunteers.

Volunteer fundraisers are your double agents. They have sat on both sides of the table. They have made commitments, and they have asked for commitments. They can open locked doors to friends and acquaintances. They can tell it to you straight without fear of self-preservation. They are a limitless source of information.

Previously, I described the universal dislike of discovery work by fundraisers. Volunteers have an easier time doing this because they do not work at the organization. Each approaches the prospect as a peer, not as a salesperson. As an example, when you travel to a new city and want to find a restaurant for dinner, are you more likely to respond to the advertisements at the hotel or to a list of favorite places a local friend suggests? Your friend is only looking out for your satisfaction, or at least would like you to experience what gave them satisfaction. When you reach out to a donor, you (the professional fundraiser) are like the restaurant ad in the hotel. The volunteer is the local friend.

A great fundraiser will leverage their personal relationships to help with initial trust transfer. If a peer trusts you, your visit is the equivalent of the local restaurant recommendation. If you maintain a two-way relationship of mutual respect with the volunteer, then they will continue to advocate on your behalf. There really is no trick to it. Effective volunteer engagement emerges from the effort you put into building a relationship with the volunteer.

COLLABORATION OUTSIDE THE ORGANIZATION

A few years back, I was conducting a feasibility study for an international NGO (non-governmental organization). I met some of the most inspirational people I have ever met. They selflessly gave to make the world better for others. The effectiveness of the organization in meeting its mission was the primary motivation for donor loyalty. These were multimillion-dollar donors with long histories of support. Even with such extraordinary giving relationships, they were enthused about one area of the case I did not expect.

The NGO included a collaboration pillar in their campaign where they would work with other nonprofits and universities to solve really big problems. These donors had no relationship to the other nonprofits and universities, but the fact that the NGO was collaborating lifted their sights. The NGO was not leveraging other brands but was, rather relentlessly, pursuing fulfilling its mission.

Donors don't give to you. Donors rarely give to your institution. They give to the hope made real in their gift. If it is a scholarship fund, they are giving to change the life of a future student. If they give to your research program, they are giving to the families spending more time with a loved one cured of a disease. If they donate land for conservation, they are embracing the joy of future generations enjoying nature. When they choose to give to you, they have decided you are a vehicle for this future hope and realized satisfaction. Your choice as an organization to collaborate for this purpose only strengthens your position.

Similarly, fundraisers at other organizations may at times compete for the same philanthropic dollar, but, most of the time, these are people just like you with a passion for improving our world. These should be your friends. If you have a donor in common, talk to each other about how to best benefit the donor. You may have an opportunity to realize a gift you couldn't even imagine. And you will build a trust with the donor that will surely pay back dividends.

DON'T GO IT ALONE

My main hobby outside of fundraising is writing music. Until recently, it was mostly a solitary activity. I would sit at a piano or at my computer and produce melodies, chord structures, instrument parts, and voice parts. Sometimes I finish the pieces, sometimes I don't. For the most part, I wrote the music not necessarily to be performed, but because I enjoyed doing it. After a while, I realized I could be better at my craft. I've always been a bit intimidated by other composers. I didn't want to accidently copy something they did. And honestly, I didn't want to be reminded how much better they were than me.

A few years ago, I decided to set aside my pride and try to improve. I started to meet with other composers. I went to Nashville a couple of times to attend songwriting classes. I became a better songwriter.

I've met many fundraisers who have no use for conferences. They tell me it's all the same old stuff every time. These same fundraisers, although sometimes quite good at their craft, still have opportunities to learn and improve. They have their own system and it works. *Why fix it if it ain't broke?* Pride may be preventing them from their own improvement.

There are opportunities to collaborate and learn all around you. From meeting with other fundraisers and development staff, to engaging with volunteers to industry peers, there is no shortage of opportunity. Give voice to the others by opening your ears. Don't go it alone. Be a collaborative fundraiser.

CHECKING THE BOXES: DIVERSITY

According to demographic data collected about the largest and most diverse metro areas in the United States, I currently live in one of the top five most diverse cities in the United States. With a population of 7 million, ethnicity is widely distributed with 28% Anglo, 19% Black, 43% Hispanic, and 10% Asian/Other. At the same time, the city's current population is getting more and more diverse as the population ages. Not only is our total population diverse, but each of our generations has a different ethnic make-up as well The Kinder Institute for Urban Research at Rice University, The 41st Kinder Houston Area Survey, May 17, 2022).

The main problem with demographic surveys is that I never fit into one box for ethnicity. I'm white, but also Hispanic—and they don't have a box for that. Even though I look Caucasian I do not identify primarily as Caucasian; I do not like to check the "white, non-Hispanic" box without also checking the Hispanic box. My grandmother went through many tribulations as a Mexican woman from Houston married to a German Norwegian man from Minnesota. She spent one winter up in Minnesota with my grandfather's family, and then told him she was moving back to Texas (with their infant daughter) and he was welcome to join them. I had always blamed the cold winter for the reason I didn't grown up in the Twin Cities, but my Minnesota family revealed that my grandmother was alone and isolated. As a young and smart Hispanic woman, there was no one up there she could relate to. None of her children or grandchildren grew up knowing Spanish or following Mexican culture, which always bothered me. But I realized that my grandmother never tried to abandon her heritage; she tried to protect her children from prejudices she or her family may have experienced by hiding or masking her heritage in white culture.

I am very proud of my Mexican heritage living down here in Texas. I come from a long line of strong, persistent women of immigrants. When I worked at a theater, one of my box office colleagues shares my grandmother's maiden name of Rodriguez—we often joked that we were related. To this day she calls me "Adelita," a Mexican warrior believed to have fought in the Revolutionary War. Women like her were soldiers who rode on horseback with rounds of bullets strapped to their chests. I guess you can say in my persistence and strength, I'm a cross between Rosie the Riveter and Adelita!

As working parents, my husband and I have intentionally exposed our daughters to diversity from a very early age at day care. We are big public school fans, not only because we had great experiences ourselves growing up, but because we want our girls to embrace diversity while still being able to maintain their values and beliefs. I love watching the world through my daughters' eyes, particularly how they interact with friends who are different than them. My nine-year-old daughter's best friend has different-colored skin than she does. The only times the girls talk about it is when they are coloring pictures of themselves. "Serena has brown skin and I have peach skin," she says. But to these young girls, skin color has nothing to do with how they view each other; it's equivalent to describing the color dresses they were wearing that day. My girls have yet to experience the biases that life brings us. What if we didn't carry biases about race and skin color, and saw each other, our colleagues, and our donors, through the eyes of a child? We must strive to be color inclusive, cognizant, kind, and respectful of anyone who looks or acts different from us.

Though equity, diversity, and inclusion definitely merit much discussion in our field, I am by no means an expert in these topics. To do them justice, entire books should be written about them for our field. To me personally and my journey as a development professional, diversity is all-encompassing—to be the best fundraisers (and people), we must also be inclusive of diversity of thought, political beliefs, economic and racial backgrounds, religious beliefs, and stages of life. When we think colleagues don't look like us or act like us, we may withdraw and not attend a professional mixer. When we think donors don't look like us or act like us, we may request that a certain donor be put into someone else's portfolio. However, it is so important for us to reach out across whatever difference we feel divides us from others in our profession and find common ground. How might we foster inclusion and acceptance with our colleagues? What are we doing as development professionals to create a diverse staff culture among our teams? We must be intentional and place equity, diversity, and inclusion at the center in our workplaces. It has been very important to me at previous positions to build and retain diverse teams. I have hired across the demographic spectrum, and it brings me joy to see a diverse team of individuals come together to achieve great things for an organization.

Working in the performing arts has introduced my family to a beautifully collaborative and diverse community of artists and staff members. In high school, theater was where I learned about empathy, inclusivity, collaboration, and community building, among others whose backgrounds were not like my own.

WOMEN IN FUNDRAISING: EQUITY

In recent years, there has been more focus and attention on pay equity in our profession. This is due in part to the creation and prioritization of the Association of Fundraising Professionals (AFP) IDEA Impact program and the Women's Impact Initiative, which are intended to serve diverse communities of fundraisers. According to AFP's *The Impact of Gender on Fundraising Salaries 2014–2018*, this is what we currently know about gender parity in fundraising pay:

• The fundraising profession suffers from a gender pay gap; controlling for other factors, a fundraiser who is a woman can expect to make about 10% less than her male counterparts.

• 42% of men work in an organization with a budget of $10 million or more, compared with one-third of women.

• Nearly 60% of men hold a high-level position, compared with 52.5% of women.

• Just 15% of men reported experiencing one or more negative factors (such as leaving a position to take care of a child), compared with more than a quarter of women (25.7%).

What I find interesting with this report is the barriers women face that create pay inequity. When I look at an issue, I like to dissect it, and then try to identify the root of the problem. I think the questions we must ask ourselves—as women, as fundraisers, and as hiring managers—are these:

• What are the key contributing factors leading to men being paid 10% more than women? Is it advanced degrees, having higher-level positions, and working for larger shops?

- Why are we as women not pursuing advanced degrees and higher positions?
- What opportunities can we as women in fundraising open up for ourselves and each other to blaze a path forward (not because we are owed it solely based on gender), but based on our awesome abilities and merit?

As a woman in fundraising, it is hard to talk about equity without talking about pay. The truth is, I was never taught as a woman how to negotiate my salary. For me, compensation is an uncomfortable subject, and something I am not necessarily motivated by. I am more motivated by the recognition, the challenge, and a sense of accomplishment. However, being from a family of four (the eldest sister of three younger brothers), I was raised with a heightened and keen sense of awareness around fairness. Though I'm not primarily motivated by pay, I do expect to be compensated fairly for what my time, experience, and credentials are worth. My husband is far better at negotiating salary and has taught me how to navigate this in my career. Women fundraisers, I would highly recommend a career coach or mentor who can help you negotiate a fair salary for your current or next position. As we know in the nonprofit field, unfortunately, sometimes pursuing a jump in salary means moving to a new position at a different nonprofit, but if your employer is wise and knows the importance of development staff turnover, they will counter and try to retain you.

Inclusive Design

To be inclusive means being all-encompassing, comprehensive, and empathetic. It means helping all, and including all, regardless of stage of life, age, gender, special needs or abilities, or accessibility needs. Inclusivity means we include all genders and races. The thing about inclusivity, equity, and diversity, is that they must be rooted in trust, transparency, communication, and compassion; not fear, distrust, or secrecy. We must practice inclusivity with internal and external stakeholders—our staff, volunteers, and leaders—and our clients, patients, or patrons. When we practice inclusivity, it helps everyone.

Let's look at inclusive design, for example. When it comes to the architecture of a building or museum, inclusive design goes far above creating accessibility; it is about helping everyone experience the building in their own way. For instance, when Americans with Disabilities Act (ADA) accessibility ramps were first created on sidewalks for those in wheelchairs, they ended up helping the elderly who used walkers and families with young children in strollers.

You may be wondering how inclusive design relates to fundraising. First, if you are launching a capital campaign for your organization, please make sure you or your architecture firm is thinking about and implementing inclusive design. Second, inclusivity principles can be applied to any and all industries. We are in the business of philanthropy, so we, as development professionals, should find our own principles of inclusivity. Perhaps principles of inclusive philanthropy could include: seeking out points of exclusion for our external stakeholders, identifying situational challenges for our donors, recognizing personal biases we have as fundraisers, offering different ways to engage our donors, providing equivalent experiences for all our donors and staff, and extending an inclusive solution to everyone at the organization. These principles of inclusive philanthropy are actually based in the key principles for inclusive design.

COGNITIVE BIAS AND
BIAS-BASED THINKING

To understand bias-based thinking we must first understand cognitive bias. We all struggle as humans with cognitive bias because it is a normal function of our brains for processing and categorizing information. However, bias-based thinking is not helpful when it influences how we hire staff or talk to or try to relate to staff, donors, or board members and other volunteers. Cognitive biases get in the way of fundraising when we *assume*. When you assume how a colleague, volunteer, or donor is thinking or feeling, unless you have literally walked in their shoes, you can't relate to their entire experience as a person.

So how do we as fundraisers, in the business of relationship building, not operate in fear of upsetting someone because we are afraid cognitive bias will creep in? We can't. We must give ourselves and others the benefit of the doubt that we are coming from a place of trust and generosity of spirit. Do what you do best as a development professional—relate and listen—and try to understand the journeys of others as donors and as individuals. We as humans have an innate desire to relate to one another and connect. On behalf of your organization, you can strive to overcome your own cognitive bias by learning (attending trainings), listening, and putting yourself in others' shoes.

COLLABORATIVE FUNDRAISING

Too many organizations work in silos instead of partnering to focus on the strength of the collective. This leaves fundraisers scrambling for funding and perhaps chasing funding for duplicate efforts within a community. Modern fundraisers focus not only on the passion of their donors, but also on what could enhance their organization and their community. They strategically collaborate with donors and with program staff to realize the fullest potential of their organization's impact in the community. They are always putting the needs of the organization and its ability to impact the community first. They are not chasing funding to create new programming, but instead strategically creating alignment between programming and funding. They are the matchmakers for the funder and their organization's programs. They collectively cultivate donors together with a shared vision and values of advancing their sector and their community at large.

When I worked at a hospital system, we undertook a collaborative fundraising initiative with the affiliated academic teaching hospital. The reason we pursued this collaborative fundraising campaign was because the donors requested it through a feasibility study. We had a shared feasibility study; shared marketing materials; shared campaign priorities, mutual campaign reporting, and many, many meetings between the two institutions that operated at very different paces. I found the entire experience incredibly fascinating, and it taught me that collaborative fundraising can exist and create successful results.

COLLECTIVE IMPACT

Funding often creates siloes and territorialism among organizations. It becomes a race for fundraisers to see who can get to a donor first. If we decide to collaborate with like-minded organizations to meaningfully fundraise and market together—or better yet, create collective impact initiatives—our funders benefit, our organizations benefit, and we benefit as fundraisers. We fundraisers are by nature connectors, so our ultimate goal should be to bring our community together with resources to create great and lasting impact.

"Collective impact is a network of community members, organizations, and institutions who advance equity by learning together, aligning, and integrating their actions to achieve population and systems level change" ("What Is Collective Impact?," Collective Impact Forum, 2022, collectiveimpactforum.org).

It is a structured approach to break down the walls that divide our organizations from one other. Collective impact is rooted in five conditions involving a common agenda, shared metrics, integrated activities, continuous communication, and a strong infrastructure or backbone. Therefore, collective impact fundraising is much harder to accomplish than collaborative fundraising and requires more coordination, more resources, more time, more communication, more transparency, and more trust, but yields greater impact.

COMMUNITY-CENTERED FUNDRAISING

In the spirit of collaboration, I would like to end this chapter with an excerpt from a blog by a colleague and thought leader I like to follow, Vu Le. Vu is a visionary leader with a heart for community building and social change in our industry. He challenges us as fundraising professionals to break down our organizational silos and go beyond donor-centric fundraising into community-centered fundraising. Here are his recommendations from his blog post "Winter is coming, and the donor-centric fundraising model must evolve":

Adopt the great stuff from donor-centric fundraising as a default. Acknowledge donors quickly, communicate frequently, don't treat people like ATMs, build relationship, appreciate every gift no matter the size, personalize, discuss impact and how donors play a role, solicit feedback, be transparent, etc.

Challenge and educate your donors. In trying constantly to make donors feel comfortable, we forget that we should sometimes make them feel uncomfortable.

Be knowledgeable about issues other than just the ones your nonprofit is working on. You don't have to be an expert, but so many issues are interrelated, and we need to break out of our silos.

Introduce donors to other nonprofits. Depending on the fundraising professional, this may be perceived as blasphemy. But I really believe that it will help us strengthen the sector, and thus the community, if we nonprofits are more supportive of and generous with one another.

Change the "you" to the "we." No, not the "we" referring to your organization—"This year, we served 300 families"— but the "We" that includes BOTH the donor and your organization working together, and the "We" that signifies all of us belonging to the same community.

—Vu Le, "Winter is coming, and the donor-centric fundraising model must evolve," *Nonprofit AF* (blog), April 20, 2015, nonprofitaf.com/2015/04/ winter-is-coming-and-the-donor-centric- fundraising-model-must-evolve/

CHAPTER DISCUSSION GUIDE

- How can you apply principles of inclusive design to your own fundraising efforts?
- How has cognitive bias or bias-based thinking affected you in the past, professionally or personally?
- What are ways your team can be more collaborative within your department or organization?
- How might you help create greater diversity and equity within our profession?
- How can you help build better community among your fellow nonprofit colleagues?
- What does community-centered fundraising mean to you?
- How might collective impact programming be implemented in your organization?

4

THE AUTHENTIC FACTOR

*I believe this fundraiser would give the same gift if they
had my money.*

—Anonymous donor

Over the past couple of decades or so, I've presented at
countless conferences and given even more web presentations. One presentation in particular stands out for me.
I was asked to substitute for a speaker who had fallen ill.
I was available and happy to jump in at the last moment. The
intended speaker had assembled a brilliant presentation. It
was full of new ideas and strategies I had not considered. Her
outline was clear, and the content was on point.

I began the presentation by introducing myself and
explaining that I was the substitute, but that I would be giving her presentation. As I went through the slides, I would
say things such as, "She suggests that you do this at this point

of the campaign" and "I think what she means here is this."
I was speaking in the third person as if I were narrating a
presentation.

I was boring myself. It was dreadful. I can only imagine
how brutal it was to listen to.

As I noted earlier, her presentation was a good one. I had
good material to work with. I have given many successful
presentations, so I don't think I am a poor presenter. Then
why was it such a train wreck?

For one thing, I wasn't speaking in my own voice. In trying
to represent her voice rather than naturally presenting with
my own, I created a veil of inauthenticity.

Have you ever been to a restaurant and thought the server
was just going through the motions? Maybe they did their
job in all the right ways, but it was clear they would rather be
somewhere else. Now compare that to meeting the chef at a
restaurant. When they speak about their dishes, they do so
with a passion that only the creator of the dish could express.

Culturally, our sense for inauthenticity is higher than ever.
We are in a moment where substance is actually stronger
than style. We value believing in someone more than we are
wowed by their big personality. Try Googling "millennials
and authenticity." You will be surprised by the volume of
studies, articles, and blog posts that appear in the search
results. Much research has revealed authenticity to be a pre-
vailing value of the younger generation. It is not only about
younger people wanting to keep it real. Honesty, even if
imperfect, is more compelling than a staged performance.

A few years ago, my team conducted a research project to
understand the drivers of successful fundraisers. We asked
fundraisers from several institutions to complete a survey,
describing it as a retention survey, which it was. But we also

had performance data for each of the fundraisers. This project was an opportunity for us to understand how personal perceptions about the job related to actual performance. We had so much data on what fundraisers did, but little on what was in their heads.

One question in the survey was a simple ranking. We asked, "What do you like the most about your job?" Possible answers included flexible work hours, mission of the organization, compensation, colleagues, and so on. During the analysis, we segmented the groups into cohorts. The top cohort was the most prolific fundraisers, representing about one-fifth of the study population and raising about four-fifths of the total dollars. This group ranked the mission of the organization as the top aspect they loved about their job. For no other cohort was this answer higher than fourth place. The most successful fundraisers cared very deeply about the mission of the organization.

We also asked the question, "Do you like your job?" Instead of a yes/no selection, we provided an open-ended response box. Curiously, the lower performing fundraisers gave simple responses such as "Yes, it's great." By contrast, the higher performing fundraisers provided multifaceted responses saying, "Let me explain what is good and what needs to change," and then went on to do so. The most successful fundraisers cared very deeply about how the organization met its mission.

That study reminded me of a project I did for about a dozen public broadcasting stations several years ago. One of our goals was to determine the drivers of giving big gifts to the station. We looked at such variables as capacity data, giving history, selected premiums, the program airing during an inbound call gift, and we questioned whether they were predictable in their patterns or asymmetrical, where they lived in the market, and so on. The top driver of major giving caught me completely by surprise.

A unique characteristic of major donors and future major donors, which we saw at a much lower rate in the random donor population, was "calling the station to make a complaint." Complaining? And to think we were sending the best donors to the interns managing the complaint lines.

If public television or public radio was just a choice for someone, then when they saw or heard something they did not like or didn't meet their standards, I suspect they just changed the channel. But for those who cared deeply about the mission of public broadcasting, they were likely to want it to continue to improve, and so they called to express their dismay about something.

Maybe we had this all wrong. Now when people called to complain, one of the staff members looked them up in the database to see if they were engaged donors. If so, the interns would forward the call to a major gift officer. In the first week of implementing this program, they closed a major gift for programming over the phone.

In a separate study a few years later, we interviewed prospects and donors assigned to major gift fundraisers. Similar to the officer retention study, we already had the data distinguishing which fundraisers were more successful than others. At this point, we knew what major gift officers did. We learned how they felt about their work. Our goal in the study was to determine how the donor perceived the major gift officers through their interactions.

Most of the donors were quite skilled in working with major gift officers. On average, each donor estimated they had about three officers representing charities they support regularly calling on them. One person said he had about 10 fundraisers, but they kept rolling over. He had a hard time keeping track of their names.

The key finding from this study was an emergent persona of the top fundraisers. The donors who not only gave the most, but were also assigned to officers who raised the most money, were most likely to say, "I believe this fundraiser would give the same gift if they had my money."

In both studies, our goals were to move beyond activities. Activities can be packaged into stuff that consulting firms like mine can easily deliver. In our analysis, these tactics vary from institution to institution because of culture, history, community, and philanthropic sector. We were pleasantly surprised that across institutions, authenticity was a much stronger driver of success than any activity. Although tactics matter, your own voice matters more. It turns out donors also found honesty, even if imperfect, was more compelling than a staged performance.

CAN PASSION BE TAUGHT?

As a fundraiser, you may be asking, If personal belief in the mission to the point of giving a gift myself is the primary driver of success, what if I lack this passion? Is it too late for me? What about for my team?

This is a challenge we should be able to solve. Fundraisers are in the propensity-building business. We cultivate relationships so we can invite prospects to give very large gifts to our mission. We do this by finding donor interests that align to organizational interests. Next, we provide exposure to these areas of our organization. Then, we get prospects involved and interacting with our organization. Finally, we know our relationship is strong when the prospect shifts from second-person to first-person pronouns (from "What you should do is . . ." to "What we should do is . . .").

If you want to be an authentic fundraiser, try following these steps on your own:

1. Find an area of your organization that relates to an interest you have. If there isn't something, then I'm not sure you are at the right place.

2. If there is some area of interest, no matter how small, learn more about that area. Go and meet the program staff and build a relationship. Dig in deep, even if it is not the area you raise money for at your organization.

3. Make a first gift to the area. The funny thing about giving is that the actual act of doing it builds propensity.

4. After you make your first gift, your affinity will grow. This is an investment in you as much as it is in the organization.

If you manage a fundraising team, think about officer cultivation strategy. And I do not mean strategies for how they cultivate donors. I'm talking about developing strategies to cultivate your officers to your charity. Be purposeful about mission exposure with your team. It is good to celebrate the gifts they close, but also celebrate the impact of these gifts. We use impact messages with donors; your team needs them too. They need to believe they have a role to play in making the world a better place. We all know the gifts wouldn't happen without them, and the impact does not happen without the gifts.

SALES TRAINING

I'm a consultant. I get it. About half of you are reading this book and thinking, "Josh just wants to sell consulting work." Hopefully, some of you know me and realize I would write this book only because I believe in what I say. I work in this profession because I believe I can make a difference in nonprofits. Their missions are worth it. My passion is the enablement of fundraisers to meet their missions. All said, yes, I do work in consulting and get to sell work. I love what I do and believe it makes a real difference.

How I train consultants has changed substantively since I first started. I don't actually teach consultants how to sell work per se. I teach them about why we exist. I focus on our mission to advance our clients and also advance nonprofits beyond our client universe, to discover new and novel approaches fitting each client specifically, and to maintain a thriving work environment where every voice matters and we view our role in philanthropy as a great honor. Then I ask them to embrace these guiding principles.

For every prospective client we meet, each consultant will make the most impact if each is committed to these aspirations in the way that fits their unique, special ability. We are not trying to give people what they don't want. We are trying to help them access what they want and need. If we don't offer what they need, we help them find one of the many other great companies committed to advancing the sector.

I would approach training major gift officers in the same way. Build a solid foundation in the guiding principles of your organization. Start by answering several key questions. Why does your organization exist? Why is it necessary for the world or your community? How will you catalyze this impact by introducing like-minded donors to your deep commitment? These guiding principles will be the fuel to meet new prospects. The discovery call will not come across as phony persuasion but as authentic enthusiasm. The donors value this authenticity more than you know. After all, there are no fundraising activities that are more effective than you believing in your purpose and speaking with your own voice.

Transparency

No one believes that you are perfect. No donor believes that your organization is perfect. You will have funded priorities that fail to work. You will miscode a gift. You will mistakenly accept a gift from someone you shouldn't have. A person in an endowed position will leave. In circumstances like these, are you willing to tell the truth to your donors, or will you sugarcoat your message?

All three of my daughters play or played high school volleyball. As volleyball parents, we all take our turns either working concessions, collecting money at the entrance to the games, or line judging. One year, I was on my way to a game and snagged the back pocket of my pants on my car door. The snag tore my pants open at the pocket enough that there was no hiding it. Needless to say, this was an embarrassing situation. Fortunately, I was wearing a jacket that day that provided just the right amount of coverage. So I attended the volleyball game and kept my jacket on the entire time.

Soon after I arrived at the gym, one of the parents found me and asked that I take my turn at line judging. I declined to serve in the role and could see that she was visibly annoyed at my response. In her mind, I was just another parent shirking his duties. "Really, how difficult is it to line judge for a junior varsity volleyball game?" she must have thought. There was no way I was going to tell her why I couldn't take off my jacket and line judge. The whole cheering section would surely notice me baring my soul—only it wouldn't be my soul!

She went on to ask someone else. The guilt grew within me. My embarrassment was building a wall between me and the other parent. This was unnecessary. Is my pride really more valuable than my connection with another person? It lasted about 10 minutes. I went back to her and told the truth.

Now I tried to laugh along with her as she found my situation quite amusing. It was embarrassing for me, but I did feel so much better. Not only that, the wall came down. We chatted a bit more at the game. I was no longer an unwilling parent. Now I was simply a regular person dealing with an embarrassing situation.

Though you hopefully won't ever have to face a similar "soul baring" situation, when you do have to be honest with donors about things that don't work, your honesty can actually strengthen the relationship. Sometimes in these situations, donors will even offer to help. By trying to stage a perfect view of your institution, you might actually be building walls.

I was asked to present on a campaign for a board of trustees for a university. They wanted to hear about the progress of the campaign and understand the obstacles we were facing. In our work leading up to the meeting, the chief development officer and I agreed that one of the challenges was within the development team. Although a few key fundraisers, including the chief development officer (CDO), were closing the lead gifts, the major gift officers were not meeting their activity metrics. We were afraid that being honest would make the program look bad. Nevertheless, we agreed that I would tell the truth about it and discuss our plan for improving the results.

When I delivered the results of our analysis, the trustees were not upset. Rather, I would say they became more engaged than ever. One board member offered to provide tips his company used to strengthen their sales team. Another member offered to help meet with the officers to renew their passion. Yet another gave tips on effective dashboard reports and tracking mechanisms. These trustees did not give to the institution because the institution was perfect. They gave because they believed in the ideals, aspirations, and purpose of the institution. In every part of their beings, their desire was to make the institution better. In setting aside our fears, we gave them the opportunity to do so.

Many boards seem to expect sanitized messages from staff and consultants. I've served on several boards myself and experienced this firsthand. For the most part, these board experiences taught me to read between the lines and decipher the coded language. A couple of organizations I've served demonstrated they would tell it to us straight. That was so refreshing. Not only did it build trust and give value to my role as a volunteer, but it made the good news even more exciting.

LEARN FROM YOUR VOLUNTEERS

In Chapter 3, I described the benefits of collaborating with volunteers. By now, it should be clear why volunteers are so successful. But let's dive into that a little more. When someone is a volunteer, their authenticity does not need to be proven. Volunteers are not motivated by metrics. They are not paid for the work, nor are they concerned about their "job." They are not worried about their turf or the competition. They only care about the mission.

Their only reward is advancing the cause they so fervently support.

As a fundraiser, you need to find the volunteer headspace for yourself. Why do you do this work? Is it just a paycheck to you? Something in you must think of it as something more. If money is your goal, I can think of much easier ways to make it.

What we do as fundraisers is really quite special. Our sector is comprised of people willingly giving money away. In an economic sense, they have found something more valuable than money. Whether it is saving the planet or preserving the arts, donors want others to have a better life. It is such an immense privilege to give this joy to our donors. Most of them perceive their gifts among the greatest accomplishments of their lives. You helped them do this.

As hokey as it may sound, try writing out a gratitude checklist. Capture why you love the work you do. List all the things that give you joy. Describe all the reasons your organization is important—to you, the community, the region, and the world. From the importance list, underline the items that really make you proud.

Next time you sit down with a prospective donor over coffee, try pulling sentiments from this list. Let them into your headspace. Demonstrate why you care. Show them why your organization is a source of real joy to you. Invite them to share your joy.

Connecting People
with Their Passions

Do what you love and love what you do. I know this phrase seems simple, but often we as fundraisers are caught working in positions for organizations we are no longer passionate about. We may find ourselves in good paying positions, but there are other nonprofits that truly make our hearts sing. We may work in development for a nonprofit for which we can successfully fundraise, but when it comes time to volunteer, we do it for another cause we are passionate about. Why can't the two coexist? Why can't we position ourselves and our careers around causes that we are so deeply passionate about?

Too often we overlook why we got into this business in the first place. It has become a business, and fundraising garners higher salaries than other areas in the nonprofit sector. Nonprofits always need fundraisers because we are essential revenue generators. And the good fundraisers are hard to find and recruit because they are either not interested in switching jobs or are being pursued by multiple institutions. For example, in less than one year, I was pursued for three senior development leadership positions. You stay in our field long enough and you don't have to apply for positions; you get recruited and can choose your own destiny.

So why do we as fundraisers settle? Perhaps because the position supports our families and our lifestyle. Perhaps because we are treated fairly and compensated well for the work we do. But the moment your position becomes a "job," you should think about leaving. We choose to work in the nonprofit space to change the world and make it a better place. We need authentic fundraisers and support staff who are passionate about their roles and the organizations they are serving.

Prior to the pandemic, I had coffee with a fundraising colleague at a university. She was traveling a lot for the university advancement team and was experiencing severe burnout. I asked her if she liked her job. She said yes, but her response lacked much conviction. But when she started reflecting on being a theater major in college and her passion for the arts, her eyes began to sparkle. I encouraged her to get back into the arts, to follow her passion. Of course, working in the arts can lead to burnout too, but I think you bounce back quicker when you are passionate about the organization and its mission. The moment we become dispassionate about the mission, we really should leave. A wise colleague once said to me that "apathy is worse than hate" when it comes to the workplace. I have found that to be true for myself and my employees. When an employee is fighting for what they believe is right for the position, that means they still care. The moment they stop caring, they should consider leaving the position and finding someplace else that needs their talents.

When people ask what I do for a living, I say I'm a professional fundraiser. Then they almost always say, "I don't know how you do that for a living. I could never ask people for money." I tell them I don't ask people for money. "I connect them with their passions."

PASSION FOR THE ORGANIZATION AND ITS MISSION

I think passion and authenticity for the organization's mission should be a requirement when hiring staff. Because of the night and weekend work required in the performing arts in addition to the normal workday, I started hiring employees first based on their passion for the arts organization. I knew that passion for the mission was a key indicator of success within the culture of the organization and in the retention of employees. As long as the prospective employee had a good baseline of development experience, I could teach everything else. Someone once told me that management is 80% hiring the right person, the rest can be taught. Conversely, hiring the wrong person who is not the right culture fit for the organization, will take 80% of your time to manage and mitigate.

During my hiatus from the arts, I remember talking with a college friend at a fundraising gala. She was a former Broadway performer who had opened up a studio in New York City. I was guilt-ridden telling her how I much I missed working in the theater. She asked me about my job at the moment; I was leading a development team for a literacy organization that provided professional development and dyslexia training so that children could learn how to read. She looked at me sideways and said, "Are you crazy?! You are doing so much good where you are now! The theater will always be here." And she was right. She has now also found a calling as a motivational speaker for Simon Sinek. Simon Sinek is a world-renowned speaker who asks his followers to "start with why." That's what I ask you today as fundraisers— what is your "why" in this profession? Why do or did you first pursue this as a career? Why do you continue to pursue this calling? Does your current position reflect your passion or current calling? And if not, why are you still there?

While working at the healthcare system, I became passionate about neurosciences because of the people involved in the project. These donors let me into their lives as we fundraised for spinal cord injury and recovery, a cause that had directly affected them. They opened up their contact list so I met their friends from childhood, university, business school, their children's school, the country club, and their employer. It was an incredible cause, so I was passionate about the project and passionate about them. Those donors became like family to me, and we are still close to this day. I loved working for the hospital because I learned the best practices in fundraising. I knew the arts would call me back at some stage, and at that point I would "return home." I even told my colleague that I would stay at the hospital as long as I could because I had proper resources and was rewarded for my success, but the moment the arts called me back, I would have to go—and I did.

Brand Ambassador

Development is so much more than a job; it becomes your life and your personal brand. One of the first keys to fundraising is being able to represent and even embody the organization for the donors and community around you. Truly successful fundraisers, and especially fundraising executives, are community organizers and resources for their organization. When I represent my organization in the community, whether it is at a Thanksgiving parade or a luncheon, I would always say, "I am Amy Lampi from [organization]." That way my identity would be linked with my organization. When you embody your organization's brand, it can help with retention with your organization, but at that moment you are also being linked as the "go-to" person for the organization. People in the community will ask you for theater tickets, to get them into a particular class, or ask you to get them in to see a certain physician or into the emergency room; you become a community resource for your institution and will need to monitor your free time wisely. The only danger about mixing community relations with development is work–life balance, meaning it often does not exist.

The truth is, when I take on a new organization, those donors do indeed become my new professional and personal network and sometimes friends. I intentionally establish the same amount of trust and transparency and authenticity as I do with my own personal friends. I don't create a separate work persona for my colleagues or donors. What you see is what you get. My life is pretty much an open book for those I decide to trust. I am vulnerable, yet strong; transparent, yet discreet. And I am always authentic, living my truth in the moment. I don't know how not to be authentic because it feels disingenuous. It is possible to live in vulnerability and authenticity as a fundraiser and to not be weak or feel exposed. Perhaps it was something I learned in acting school, perhaps it was something I have learned over time. There is incredible inner strength in humility and vulnerability; it just takes practice.

Donors as Friends

Over the years, my husband and I would return to some of my previous employers to volunteer at their major special events or galas. We have loved the donors we have met along my career journey. They have become friends and family to us. We have met their friends and their family. We've been invited to their Christmas parties, to their vacation homes, to lunches and dinners. I have gone to spas, the symphony, the opera, and the theater with them, supported their other organization's galas and luncheons, and seen them at the theater.

I recall a colleague saying that we should never be friends with our donors because the moment we leave the organization, the donors leave. I don't necessarily find that to be true, but I think if you recruit your personal friends to the institution, that could be the case. By the way, it is okay to recruit your personal friends to the institution, but only if they are truly passionate about your institution. I find it very hard to do my job successfully without being friends with my donors. The basis of friendship is trust, and the tools for building trust are transparency, authenticity, and time. Therefore, as you build trust with your donors, it is almost impossible as an authentic fundraiser to not also build a friendship. The delicate balance is to make sure the donor stays with the organization even if you decide to leave the organization.

WHY WE DO WHAT WE DO

At another theater where I was employed, on days when I was feeling worn out or defeated, the artistic director would invite me to come down to watch rehearsal of an upcoming musical. There was nothing better than that for reconnecting my fundraising soul to the mission. It always brought me out of my blues and reminded me why I was so passionate about the organization. I tried to encourage my fundraising staffs to do the same. Spend time with the program staff and listen to them talk about the incredible impact they are having in the community. Allocate time to go on site visits to see the work being done firsthand by the program staff. Sit in on a rehearsal. Audit or visit a class at the university. Go on rounds or watch a surgery for the physician whose service line you are supporting. Better yet, take a donor along with you and watch as together you spark the joy in being involved with the organization.

In closing, were you someone who was passionate at one point, but have you lost your passion along the way due to burnout? Perhaps you are still passionate about the mission, but the work environment is dysfunctional or chaotic. Maybe you have yet to find your passion. If so, look to your college major or find a hobby or an extracurricular activity you loved when you were younger. Whatever is the fastest way for you to get back to your passion, do it! We need fundraisers in the field who are passionate about their work and who bring donors alongside them for the ride. People will always give to people, and when those people are passionate and authentic about their work, it brings joy to the donors and their fellow colleagues. It makes the work not feel like work in the end.

CHAPTER DISCUSSION GUIDE

- Gratitude checklist: Take a moment to list 10 things you are thankful for about your organization.

- Why are you passionate about the cause or mission of the organization in which you are fundraising?

- Would you give the same gift to your organization if you had the money? Why or why not?

- What do you like the most about your job? Why do you do this work?

- If you could do anything for a career (regardless of money or time restrictions), what would it be?

- Are you able to recite your mission statement right now from memory?

- When you are outside of work, what is the elevator speech you give to family and friends about your nonprofit or cause?

- What do you tell friends and family that you do for a living?

5

THE CONFIDENT FACTOR

So, first of all, let me assert my firm belief that the only thing we have to fear is fear itself—nameless, unreasoning, unjustified terror which paralyzes needed efforts to convert retreat into advance.
—Franklin D. Roosevelt

As a father of daughters, I've read the Harry Potter books and watched all the movies more times than I can count. Truth be told, I am a nerd of the highest order. I would have watched them regardless of my parental role. The underpinning of the entire saga is what makes Harry Potter such a great wizard. He is not the most gifted with knowledge or intelligence. That certainly falls to his friend, Hermione Granger. He is not the most powerful. That honor would fall to Professor Dumbledore or Lord

Voldemort. Instead, Harry's best attribute is his bravery. Harry does what needs to be done even if it is really scary. Harry is, perhaps, the bravest wizard of them all.

But is bravery enough? My favorite quote from Harry Potter is from *The Order of the Phoenix*. His friends are trying to convince the other students why Harry is such a great wizard. They list his many accomplishments like defeating dementors, facing Voldemort, killing a mighty basilisk and so on. Harry's response was, "Wait . . . look, it all sounds 'great' when you say it like that. But the truth is most of that was just luck. I didn't know what I was doing half the time, I nearly always had help. . ."

While I'm not going to ever meet Harry Potter, I have met many of the greatest fundraisers in the United States and around the world. Several have closed transformational gifts for their institutions; some of these gifts exceeded $100 million. They found audiences with captains of industry. They were behind amazing building projects. They generated funding for new medical procedures that saved thousands of lives. Their work lifted communities out of poverty. When I asked them how they did it, their answers were basically very Harry Potter-like, "Wait . . . look, it all sounds 'great' when you say it like that. But the truth is most of that was just luck. I didn't know what I was doing half the time, I nearly always had help. . ."

Why does this type of "luck" seem to follow the same people? What gives them the bravery to boldly go forward when they don't have all the answers? Why do some people seem to just do it?

Over the years, my team has conducted several studies to weigh activity metrics for our clients. Using the techniques of relationship modeling outlined in Chapter 1, we looked at the things fundraisers did. Then we compared and contrasted methods employed by the most productive fundraisers.

Across institutions, the most common measurable factor that distinguishes successful fundraisers from their colleagues is solicitation levels. Top fundraisers will ask for a higher amount as a ratio to capacity. We combined these findings from seven separate client studies, four of which were for healthcare institutions and three were for universities. We found that the bottom 80% of fundraisers by money raised had average asks of 44% of their internal capacity ratings. In other words, the prospect research team rated the prospects at one level, but when the fundraiser asked for a gift, the level was generally lower than the rating by more than half. When the top 20% of fundraisers asked for a gift, their average ask was just over 100% of the rating.

After our qualitative interviews, we classified the two groups as the best gift fundraisers and the lower performing gift fundraisers. The lower performing fundraisers were more likely to say, "Research says this donor can give $100K. I think the next ask should be $50K, and we work our way up." The higher performing fundraisers were more likely to say, "Research says this donor can give $100K. I start by thinking, 'What would it take for them to give $100K?'" In other words, they were trying to determine how to get the best gift from each donor.

The choice in this pursuit is grounded in bravery. Asking at capacity is bold. To do that, I would need to be prepared, I'd need some help, and hopefully, I'd get a little luck. In my observation, luck follows the prepared, and success follows the brave.

The preparation for bold asking is the sum of all of the chapters of this book. A few of the tactics bold fundraisers use are best gift strategy design, expanded blending versatility, input from others, relentless alignment, and partner involvement.

1. *Best Gift Strategy Design*

When officers make discovery calls, they are mainly focused on learning about the prospects. What drives them? Are they philanthropic? Why do they give? How do they give? How collaborative is the family unit in making philanthropic decisions? How do they feel about my organization? How involved are they with my organization? What does that engagement look like? What are their interests? Does the rating seem to accurately reflect their ultimate capability?

If, following the discovery call, the officer decides to pursue the prospect, these confident fundraisers will begin with the question, "What would it take for this prospect to give a gift at their capacity?" They might write down a strategy on a piece of paper. Certainly, the strategy will be in their head. Hopefully, it will find its way into the database.

The strategy may start with, "For this prospect to give their best gift, we would have to. . ." The strategy would capture their motivations and drivers and how the organization would rise to meet these motivations and drivers. It would describe steps to build philanthropic propensity. Perhaps the officer would capture who else in the organization needs to be involved based on the complexity of the prospect's giving patterns. It would outline key family members who need to be involved. It might incorporate organizational warming strategies to build supplemental affinity. Certainly, the strategy would list program officers, faculty, or staff who need to meet the prospect. There would be strategies for exposure to aligned interest areas. And, it would suggest an estimated timeline.

I've met with organizations that conduct many meetings about a mailing that might bring in $100K or an event that barely covers its expenses. But the same organization will have almost no planning for a single donor who can give $1 million. Bold fundraisers put as much effort into strategy for one big gift as programs do for volume-based efforts.

2. *Expanded Blending Versatility*

Very few transformational gifts are made with a simple cash transaction. Although a donor with emerging philanthropic maturity will start by writing a check, liquid cash is only one source of funding the gift. As officers and donors mature, they will begin to blend gifts into outright and deferred giving. Perhaps some portion of the gift will be in cash, while another will be a charitable bequest.

Affluent individuals have many more sources of wealth that can be gifted. Business owners have access to employee giving, corporate sponsorship dollars, corporate philanthropy, in-kind transactions, stock transfers, exit capital, and more.

In 2019, the brilliant entrepreneur and jeweler Kendra Scott funded the Kendra Scott Women's Entrepreneurial Leadership Institute at the University of Texas at Austin. This transformational gift had only one portion of the gift that was in outright cash. Ms. Scott made a personal contribution of $1 million. The other components included a programming investment of $500,000 and 20% of proceeds from product line in addition to matching funds from the University. By expanding the blended options beyond her personal cash, Kendra Scott did so much more for the institution.

Confidence in presenting expanded blending options suggests you learn about different types of assets and funding options. Invite constituents from different industries to talk about their businesses. Ask board members to help decipher the codes of the affluent. Attend a training class on entrepreneurship or business funding. Think about how you might advise a donor to give more than even they thought possible.

3. *Input from Others*

In Chapter 3, I described how great fundraisers meet with their prospect development and donor relations colleagues more often than other fundraisers. This is not only because they are good people; it's because it's a very strategic choice.

Of all the departments in a modern fundraising organization, I am most impressed by the growth in maturity of prospect development. Prospect researchers, prospect relationship management officers, and prospecting analysts have devoted their careers to helping major gift officers. If a fundraiser is Spiderman, prospect development is Ned Leeds, the "man in the chair." Your prospect development team can give you ideas for every area of your strategy. They likely have the strongest command of complex assets. They can find examples for ways the prospect or other donors like the prospect have made gifts in the past. They can locate key family members as associates. And they can help inform timing.

Donor relations professionals can help you plan your donor experience management strategy. The best future major gift donors are your previous major gift donors. This team exists to be sure each donor gets the best "TLC" your organization is able to provide. Donor journeys are long. The details are beyond you. Accept their help.

Leverage the knowledge and assistance from other fundraisers, program staff, and leadership. Don't neglect your administrative staff. Oftentimes, I've found executive assistants of donors have as strong a relationship with the fundraiser's admin as the fundraiser has with the donor. There is much insight to be found all around you.

4. *Relentless Alignment*

As a parent, I love to give my children gifts. In our household, we normally give gifts at Christmas and for birthdays. As the gift giver, I want to know what my children really want. I may even ask them directly. When they say, "Just give me money," I am a little bit disappointed. It's not really all that fun to just give money. It is much more fun to give them something specific and meaningful.

When you ask for donors to give without articulating a specific reason, it is a little bit less fun for them too. When the donor's interests and the organization's gift opportunities align, there is great joy in the transaction. It is often said, "Big gifts are given to big ideas." I think it is more accurate to say, "Big gifts are given to the *right* ideas." In my first book, *Fundraising Analytics: Using*

Data to Guide Strategy (Wiley, 2008), I introduced the idea of a value portfolio. Research indicated that major philanthropy is, psychologically, very closely related to investment. The value portfolio was a method of taking inventory of a donor's past giving, volunteering, and statements. From this inventory, one would classify how they invest their philanthropic capital. The purpose was to understand which investment options to present to them. The return would not be financial. Instead, the donor would be paid back in their value portfolio. Impact is the donor's dividend.

There is no more effective way to understand a donor's interests than through conversation. Beginning with the discovery call, find out what drives the donor. Find the people and programs most aligned to this interest. It is never perfect, but the closer the better. Be relentless in aligning donor interests with organizational interests. Once you find alignment, the donor is no longer giving you money. Instead, they are funding their own interests. These are the *right* ideas generating big gifts.

PARTNER INVOLVEMENT

In 2019, I wrote the paper "Consuming Philanthropy: How Principal, Major, Mid-Level, and Base Donors Give Differently" (BWF, September 29, 2019). My purpose was to show that people give much like we spend. Small gifts are like buying things on Amazon. We do not need a personal relationship, but we value consistency, loyalty, and ease of transaction. When we reach the four- and five-figure levels (US dollars), we begin to seek out personal contact. Although we like to talk directly with a person at a mobile phone store or car dealership before spending that much money on a purchase, we do not require a deep relationship with the salesperson. Major giving is more like buying a house. In this case, we *do* want the realtor to know our interests, show us properties in our price range that meet most of the interests, and help us with the transaction. Transformational gifts are more like mergers and acquisitions. If we are buying a company, we want to meet the people, know where it is going, determine whether we believe in it, and examine the books.

Transformational gifts rarely happen without being an open book. If you are cultivating a principal gift for Alzheimer's research, your donor will need to meet the researcher. If you hope this donor provides the lead campaign gift, they should know your president. If you are asking a donor to endow the artistic director of your theater, it might be a good idea to introduce the donor to the artistic director. If you are hoping your top donor will fund your water and sanitation project in Zambia, you should think about booking some flights and getting them on the ground.

Key partners in your organization are confidence multipliers. Your boldness can flow out of their passion. Don't expect them to be slick salespeople. Ask them to be their authentic selves. Let them say why they do what they do and explain what they hope to accomplish. They are not selling gifts, they are letting the donor into their world.

FUNDRAISING IS A CHOICE

The more I work in this space, the more I realize that this really is an effort business. The most successful fundraisers choose to be the most successful fundraisers. Luck follows the people who seek it.

If I wanted to learn a foreign language, I could take the time to do so. There is no doubt it would be a lot of work. Maybe I would take a class. Maybe I would find a tutor. I would have to start at the beginning. The more willing I'd be to put myself out there and mess up, the easier it would be for my tutor to correct me. Over time, I may even achieve mastery.

My wife's sister, husband, and family moved from the United States to Taiwan and lived there for about a decade. Although both my brother-in-law and sister-in-law built a strong command of Mandarin, I was struck by how my sister-in-law gained her skills. She went into the markets and into the community and just talked with people. Even though her skills would have been rough at first, by putting herself out there, she learned.

This is bravery. Having the strength to face fear and difficulty, but doing it nonetheless. The ability to make the brave choice is one of self-esteem. In fundraising, we can lean on both our own esteem and our organization's. This esteem is connected to worthiness.

Is my organization worthy of this gift? Am I a worthy representative of my institution?

If you have not worked at an elite charity, you might think it is easy. Of course, it's easy to ask for $10 million for Harvard—they're Harvard, after all. There is some truth to this. This is an assessment of organizational esteem.

The philanthropic consumer does brand elite institutions as the types of places to which big gifts are given. It also brands some charities as the places you give smaller monthly gifts. If you think of this from the investment lens, it makes perfect sense. Some companies are very successful at attracting investors. Jim Cramer of CNBC's *Mad Money* coined the acronym "FAANG stocks" for these types of companies. Facebook, Apple, Amazon, Netflix, and Google are very popular stocks. Over the years, they have felt like a sure investment because of their success and branding.

A local start-up might need your investment income more than Amazon does. But why would you buy the Amazon stock instead of giving to the start-up? You are making a choice based on the likelihood for a good return on the investment. Giving to small charities can feel similar. But many start-ups are funded by the right investors. It is key to find the right investors for your organization.

In my paper "Principal Gifts: Why Malcolm Gladwell Is Only Half Right" (BWF, June 24, 2019), I tried to break down this concept using Gladwell's own words. He described the concepts of "weakest link" and "strongest link." He explained that basketball is a strongest-link sport. The strength of the best player is the most predictive of the team's success. He contrasted this with soccer (or football as most of the world calls it), which he described as a weakest-link sport. In soccer, the weakest player on the team is the most predictive of the team's success. The risk of giving up a goal is a bigger driver of losing than scoring a goal is a predictor of winning. Economically, he points out correctly, that education is a weakest-link field. How well the least of a community is educated is the most predictive of the economic success of that community.

With this premise, it seemed absurd that a donor would give to an elite educational institution instead of a community-based institution. However, solving problems is a strongest-link field. Elite institutions are petri dishes for growing solutions. Creating new things, research, and ripple-effect methodologies are all strongest-link concepts. If you want to find a cure for a disease, it makes more sense to focus the capital on the researcher closest to solving the problem. Spreading the money around is less effective in finding solutions.

To a major donor, elite institutions are FAANG stocks and the strongest links for solving problems. If you do not work at one of these places, hope is not lost. Instead, you need to understand and embrace your organization's worthiness. One way is to take an inventory of a few things you do better than everyone else. In healthcare there is a term called "destination medicine." This describes areas in which people will drive or fly past their local hospital to receive unique or specialty care. What are your destination programs? I've yet to find a nonprofit that doesn't have a few points of pride to appeal to the strongest-link donor.

Often successful implementation and demonstrated impact are enough to show your worth. This is where authenticity and boldness come together. In seeking the right investor for your philanthropic program, you will need to own your organization's worth and esteem. Cultivate your own passion for the organization. If you authentically believe this, sharing your passion will not seem like a job.

Ultimately, I think *luck* is just another word for *caring enough to try*. These brave fundraisers cared enough about their missions, believed their institutions could do what they said they would do, and knew the prospective donors would find joy by coming along for the ride. You are a representative of your organization's worth.

The Princess Obsession

When I see the word *brave* I immediately think of princesses. My two young daughters, especially my younger one, are obsessed with princesses. We all went to a Disney park when my daughter turned three. I had a week-long conference, so for five days my mother and husband took the girls to the park. My husband grew up going to the parks every year, so this was a dream for him. He had every day perfectly synchronized; they never had to wait for more than 20 minutes for the next activity or ride. They went from princess appearance to princess appearance and have the autographed photo book to prove it. I do not remember the craze around Disney princesses when I was younger, but Ariel has been my favorite princess since I was a girl. So why are these little ones today so obsessed with princesses? I would wager that it is not because of their pretty and sparkly dresses; it's because they are strong women who all overcome an obstacle. Each of these princesses have no room for fear—they all must be *brave*! How might we translate that into our own development careers? How might you champion and fight for the cause for which you are raising philanthropic dollars? How might you be brave and more courageous in your advancement position as you fight for resources for you or your team?

Why Fear?

Being brave doesn't mean overcoming fear; it's about standing up in front of it. As Franklin D. Roosevelt so famously stated, "the only thing we have to fear is fear itself." When we let fear become a motivating factor, we don't take risks and therefore can't grow as development professionals. Fundraisers who are too risk averse are fearful. One must tackle that fear and understand its origins.

My older daughter had developed a phobia of elevators, which made shopping quite difficult. Whenever we were in a department store or mall, she insisted on using the escalator, which I frankly find more dangerous. For some reason, she thought she would be caught in an elevator and not be able to get out. I told her that rarely happens. (Although it did happen to me at work once when I was pregnant with her.) One way we have been able to overcome her fear is to make elevators a game—she gets to press the buttons letting passengers on and off. I also started encouraging her that if other passengers are getting on, we are not alone and will be fine because we are all together.

Bottom line, whatever feeling or phobia your fear is based on, find it, claim it, reason with it, and then conquer it! Fear has no business in fundraising. If you go into a donor meeting knowing that donor or funder is on your side and has the capacity and inclination to do so, why fear? Once you conquer the fear, it is time to move on and take some risks.

FEAR OF REJECTION

Because of my background in the theater, I do not have a fear of public speaking as others colleagues may have. We as actors learned to power through that fear very early on in our training. How that translates into fundraising is getting over the fear of rejection. As a fundraiser, I try to never make rejection an option. As an actor, you must get over the fear of rejection during the audition process. Like trained musicians, actors' bodies and voices are their "instruments," so they get used to being judged the moment they walk into the audition room. I encourage any fundraiser to take part in an audition; you will get over your fear of public speaking very quickly! My friend is a casting director and can tell in the first 30 seconds of an audition if an actor is right for a role. Her incredible casting skills have been honed and refined from seeing literally thousands of actors over her career casting regionally and on Broadway. Therefore, I think former performers make some of the best fundraisers because we know how to adapt, react, empathize, and be fearless and vulnerable all at once.

No-Fear Fundraising

My friend Gregory Robertson is the chief advancement officer at Houston Grand Opera. Greg is a masterful fundraiser and knows the art of major and principal gift fundraising better than most anyone I know. He gives an inspiring talk on "no-fear fundraising" and contributed some thoughts below:

> Fear is one of the most powerful human emotions. Some fear is instinctual and healthy and keeps us alert to trouble. The rest— the fear that holds us back from growth—is destructive and can profoundly influence our lives. There are good fears and bad fears. Common fears we experience include aging, making decisions, being alone, making friends, dying, changing jobs, rejection, loss of finances, children leaving the house, and loss of one's image. We as fundraisers cannot escape fear, but we can learn to manage it. Here are some streetwise, practical strategies to minimize the fears of your donors and those irrational fears that limit and undermine your professional success.
>
> **Donor Fears**
>
> - *The Surprise Ask:* "You are going to surprise me and ask me for money when I am not expecting it." We conquer this donor fear by being very transparent about time, agenda, and outcome prior to meeting with the donor.

- *Pressure:* "I'm going to be pressured into doing something that I don't want to do." As fundraisers, we must give donors the permission to say no to our ask.
- *Finances:* "Can I afford to make this gift?" You must anchor the ask and give donors payment options such as a flexible payment schedule or different giving vehicles.
- *Trust:* "You are not going to do what you said you would do with my money." We must keep our word with our funders and build a strong foundation of trust.
- *Doubt:* "Is my giving really making a difference?" ASK, THANK, REPORT (and REPEAT)!

Fundraiser Fears

- *Asking for Help:* It takes a lot of courage to admit that you can't do something. Most fundraisers fear rejection. We battle ego and struggle with unproductive thoughts such as: "My colleagues or donors will think I am dumb." "My colleagues or donors think I am weak." "My colleagues or donors will question my abilities." We are not expected to know everything as fundraisers. It's important to remember that great managers and leaders always ask for help.
- *Asking for Money:* We are taught at a young age that it is not polite to talk about money. Wealthy people talk about money all the time! They are okay with money conversations. Also, they know what we do for a living, so they almost come to expect it. As fundraisers, we sometimes fear being too aggressive or are scared they will say no. Nobody likes to be rejected, so we must learn that we can't take it personally. We are called to help people achieve greatness in their lives through philanthropy. It's not about raising money. People want and need to give. You are helping them facilitate that vision.
- *Being Vulnerable:* We put on a strong face to our donors and many times don't share our challenges and disappointments, but donors can handle the truth. Our donors

know that we and our organizations aren't perfect. Not everything we do is world-class, works as planned, or works well. We must stop playing it emotionally safe as fundraisers and be vulnerable and real.

POSITIVITY IN FUNDRAISING

I once gave a presentation at an Opera Conference roundtable. I had just seen the opera *Saul* the evening before and was so impacted by the piece. Contributed revenue can be 70% to 80% of what keeps operas alive in our country today, so I got choked up realizing that without fundraising, Houston residents would not have been able to see that new opera in our city. What we do as fundraisers is so important and meaningful. We must encourage and lift each other up to keep striving ahead in positivity. It is incredibly essential to applaud each other and say "Bravo! What you do is important."

We need more positivity in our profession. Next time you meet with development colleagues, make a conscious effort to be positive and see how that affects your conversation. Send an unexpected note of encouragement to a colleague at their home. We all need to be reminded that "what we do matters."

THE CHARISMA EFFECT

I read an article in *The New York Times* by author Bryan Clark about the characteristics of leadership, with a focus on breaking down the components of charismatic leadership. We are each naturally drawn to certain people. Perhaps their particular personality meshes with ours or perhaps it is their horoscope sign or Enneagram number. Whatever the reason, these particular people are magnetic to us. They also know how to adapt, read, and react well to social cues and body language. This also happens to be a key characteristic of an expert fundraiser.

There are three pillars of charisma as outlined in *The Charisma Myth*, a book by Olivia Fox Cabane (Portfolio Penguin, 2013):

1. The *presence* pillar, which involves residing in the moment and being aware of the distractions that may keep you from being present.
2. The *power* pillar, which involves breaking down the self-imposed barriers to your success such as self-doubt and imposter syndrome and "assuring yourself that you belong and that your skills and passions are valuable and interesting to others."
3. The *warmth* pillar, which invokes a feeling of kindness and acceptance, as though you are a close friend but may have just met.

Perhaps it's a trained technique I learned in acting conservatory, but the warmth pillar is the easiest for me. I am one of those people who has "never met a stranger." I need to work on the presence pillar as I get distracted easily by noises, lights, and sometimes my own thoughts. I think the pillar I could most easily work on is the power pillar. I often doubt and downplay my own expertise. I feel this pillar is thrust upon me sometimes by others in my field instead of my taking ownership of it. I often struggle with imposter syndrome and self-doubt, even in writing this book.

GRIT IN FUNDRAISING

Angela Duckworth, author of *Grit: The Power of Passion and Perseverance* (Scribner, 2016), defines grit as a blend of passion and perseverance. Passion and perseverance are character traits that are critical to the fundraiser. Passion cannot be taught, but it can be found and learned in the mission of the organization you serve. I did not realize I had a passion for neurosciences or dyslexia training for teachers, but understanding the people we served and getting to know those providing the service or skill fueled my interest and commitment to the cause and allowed me to become passionate about the mission.

Most of us have fallen into our profession of fundraising. We do not initially set out to become fundraising professionals when starting college or our careers. It is a skill we learn and hone firsthand from on-the-job training, and then it becomes a craft and talent we refine over time. You realized either quickly that "you are good at this" and have come to enjoy it. But fundraising takes serious grit. Through perseverance, we as fundraisers must sustain ourselves through the highs and lows of our profession. We must be resilient to the major gift solicitation that does not pan out, carry hope for the increased ask from a funder, or sustain ourselves through an organizational leadership transition.

If we are already defeated, can we change? Yes! Through practicing grit daily and taking charge of our passion, purposes, and perseverance, we can develop habits that will lead to ultimate changes in our character as fundraisers. According to Angela, "One form of perseverance is the daily discipline of trying to do things better than we did yesterday." Through the daily habit of showing up for work and trying to do my job when I felt like quitting, I developed grit and persistence. It is so easy for us as fundraisers to flee to the next role because we know that organizations are always hiring good fundraisers. But as a wise colleague once told me, it is better to run *toward* something than to run away from it. I learned through difficult work circumstances that developing perseverance not only developed my character, it was one of the takeaways from those positions.

PERSISTENCE IN OUR PROFESSION

We must stay the course and run the fundraising race with perseverance. It is incredibly hard. I know. I have run it with you, side-by-side, for over 20 years at various nonprofits. I know how burned out you get. I know how you want to quit. I know you sometimes question leaving the sector altogether. I know you never have enough resources or time or staff. Just don't stop. Keep running the race because our nonprofits depend on us to succeed. Don't stop until you've left your nonprofit in better shape than when you arrived. Don't stop until the goal has been achieved. Don't stop until you have empowered others to keep going. Don't stop until you've learned something new.

REJUVENATION

A colleague once said that burnout is inevitable, but it is reinvigoration that is key to combating and recovering from burnout. Rejuvenation reminds us why we care about what we do. A board member once gave me and my family the keys to her beach home for the weekend. I had accidentally left my phone at home, so I was truly able to unplug. It was after that weekend, uninterrupted with my family, that I was reminded of what truly matters in life, and I was able to rejuvenate and keep going. Find the hobbies or vacation spots that force you to unplug and enjoy life beyond work. I have had staff feel they could not leave to go on vacation, which is ludicrous. We should all be able to take time to leave and recharge. The work will always be there. Therefore, it is essential to build contingency plans at work so others can cover for you while you are away on vacation or after you leave the position.

PRIDE IN OUR PROFESSION

Fundraising is not a dirty word. Nothing makes my blood boil more than to hear negative comments about our worthy profession from those who do not truly understand what fundraising is, can be, or should be. I will never apologize for being a fundraiser. It is an incredibly noble profession. It is hard work and many times thankless. But our organizations cannot survive without philanthropy. Therefore, our industry is completely essential to the ecosystem of nonprofits. We have a higher purpose, a higher calling, to serve a greater good for our industry. If we are not proud of our profession, how can we inspire confidence in our donors to support our organizations' missions? Have you been to a restaurant and asked the server what he recommends off the menu? Many times, I will be persuaded by the server's recommendation if I can't decide what to order and they are persuasive. If they are not proud of the food they are serving or haven't tried the food, how likely are you to be confident in the food you are about to consume? We must have full assurance and confidence in the mission and the programs we are delivering to the community. We must (1) be proud of our organization's mission, but also (2) proud of what we do as fundraising professionals on a regular basis.

CHAPTER DISCUSSION GUIDE

- Why are you proud to be a fundraiser? Name a moment when you were most proud of your profession.
- After reading the section on no-fear fundraising, what strategies will you take away or develop on your own?
- Think of a time when you had to persist under difficult circumstances at a position. What made you stay? What did you learn most about yourself at the time? How did it develop your character as a fundraiser?
- If you could aspire to be a charismatic leader, which pillar type would you be and why?
- Take a moment to take Angela Duckworth's quick quiz at angeladuckworth.com to measure your own grit. How "gritty" are you as a fundraiser?

6

THE ADVOCACY FACTOR

The ones who are crazy enough to think they can change the world are the ones who do.

—Steve Jobs

Looking back now, I see that I achieved my career success because several amazing people made a choice to advocate on my behalf.

My undergraduate degree was in music. When I was first married, I was planning to begin a PhD program in composition. I was accepted and registered for my classes. However, I was waffling, considering whether or not to take a gap year or work a little first. I met with the late Dean Larry Gorrell of St. Mary's University, who at the time was the department head for their arts management program. He introduced me to the nonprofit sector and the value of administration, fundraising, and marketing for the advancement of the arts.

After ultimately enrolling in Larry's grad program, I landed an internship at the University of Minnesota. Mary Hicks, who led fundraising for the College of Liberal Arts at the time, had told the grad program of her willingness to take on interns and introduce them to the fundraising profession. Mary gave me the project of analyzing the band program and the marching band program at the University. My mandate was to provide a plan to not only build the program but to also advance its financial support. I'm afraid to look back at my analysis, but in my memory, it was a brilliant project. In reality, it may have been a bit elementary.

Nevertheless, Mary offered me a job right out of grad school. I remember her saying, "Your future is in fundraising. You may not know it yet. We can put you on the payroll. If you find something better, you should pursue it." I can't thank her enough for taking a chance on me, a grad student who still had a lot to learn.

My position with the College of Liberal Arts turned into a pathway for my progression to the central foundation of the University. In those early years, I began to formulate our first foray into data science. I was fortunate to be an early adopter in a field that took off in the next decade. An early supervisor at the foundation and driving force for our analytics journey, Randy Bunney, encouraged me to share our findings by speaking at professional associations such as CASE (Council for Advancement and Support of Education) and Apra (at the time, the Association of Professional Researchers for Advancement). Shelby Radcliffe, now the chief development officer at Willamette University invited me to speak at the first conference devoted to the concept of analytics. Things began to hum.

My early speaking gigs gave me exposure to new ideas. There was no better way to learn about a topic than by agreeing to present it to others. Assembling the slides was not nearly as stressful as preparing for the Q&A at the end of the talk. I also began to volunteer with our local chapters. After making the jump to consulting in 2004, I joined some additional committees, including the Fundraising Effectiveness Project for AFP (Association of Fundraising Professionals). At the time, I thought the exposure would be good for selling consulting work. I did not realize the committee work would be a rewarding end to itself.

Now, after more than two decades of industry speaking and participation, I continue to learn from selfless fundraisers throughout the industry. In my board role at the Giving Institute, I benefit from other business leaders committed to the industry. In chairing the Advisory Council on Methodology and Board for the Giving USA Foundation, I've had access to the brightest minds across all verticals of philanthropy. Working with the researchers at the Lilly School of Philanthropy at IUPUI and collaborating with Rice University as an instructor and advisor gives me the chance to give back to the incubator that produced me.

I was the recipient of great generosity. From Larry to Mary, and from Randy to Shelby, so many people advocated on behalf of the sector. And they advocated on my behalf. This is what great fundraisers do.

AN ADVOCATE FOR THE INDUSTRY

As a consultant, I've trained or advised countless professionals as they transition from another industry into advancement. What strikes so many of these people early on is the sharing nature of our associations. In most industries, the trade associations provide opportunities for learning and for vendors to sell their goods and services. But the networking is cautious. Beyond looking for new jobs, there is a guarded nature to meeting with competitors.

In fundraising, competition is not that formidable. There are a few cases where two nonprofits compete for the same gift. As I described in Chapter 3, donors prefer less competition and more collaboration. For the most part, we are all doing the same things and face the same challenges. Our industry has a good track record of putting our heads together for the greater good.

The trade associations provide a valuable opportunity for growth. Take the opportunity to volunteer and refine your skills as a fundraiser. Through the committee work, you will meet new friends and be exposed to new ideas. Speaking on a topic will encourage you to study and refine your craft. Networking at a conference will give you a safe zone to build your interpersonal skills and find out how other programs operate.

There is an even more compelling reason to expand your horizons. We are in the field of generosity. Everything we do is about giving. We teach donors how to give for the first time. We teach donors how to mature in their giving journey. We invite constituents to volunteer for campaigns or special initiatives. We make our own gifts to the employee campaign. Getting involved is a way for you to practice generosity and fill your authenticity tank.

An Advocate for Your Organization

For the most successful charities, fundraising is an organization-wide activity. You will not hear any us-versus-them between the program staff and the development staff. Researchers are honored to meet with prospective donors for their work. Leadership commits time and faithful interest in advancement. Artistic directors, field staff, deans, and doctors provide bold new ideas for consideration. Everyone thinks of the donor community as part of the organization and a critical variable for meeting the mission.

It might not be that way for you, yet. But building a culture of philanthropy throughout your organization is within your reach.

As a professional propensity builder, begin by crafting a cultivation strategy for your organization. I might use a task force of development professionals and a few champions outside of development. Start with the big buckets like leadership, program staff, finance, governing board (if separate from a foundation or advancement board), and so on. For each group, write down the desired future state. Next, begin to list the steps necessary to reach this future state, no matter how long or how difficult. Use all the tools at your disposal such as marketing, direct response, personal assignment, portfolios, experience management, and influencers. Then, put together an initial work plan and get to work. It will not be an overnight success. Many organizations take years to build this culture.

Let's say we are an international relief and development organization. And let's imagine our field workers located around the world find hosting donors to be the most distracting and annoying part of their job. Perhaps they even actively resist meeting with the donors. Let's also consider that donors visiting the sites in person is the single biggest driver of lifetime giving. To raise more money, we need to have willing participants in the field. In this situation, both sides may have extremely valid points.

Field workers have very difficult, time consuming, and sometimes dangerous jobs. It may take many years to develop a nuanced understanding of the culture enough to earn the trust of the recipient community. Having donors with little to no field experience travel from another country and insert themselves into the mix is not without risks. Will they say the wrong thing? Will they come in with preconceived ideas and perceptions that cloud their observations? Is there even time to handhold the donors when busy with so many other obligations?

From the fundraising perspective, donors give so much more if they can see the impact firsthand. The field workers are in their position because donors, like the ones visiting, have funded their positions. Donors are not banks. They are part of the mission ecosystem. A visit to the field may be a life-changing or life-enhancing experience for them, even solidifying a lifetime commitment of support.

The field workers and the fundraisers both have valuable perspectives. But these perspectives aren't compatible. So what do we do?

I would begin with a rigorous discovery process. For the field team, I would survey many of them and talk personally to a select portion. The goal is to capture their perspective without influencing or leading them in a certain direction. It is important that they can articulate their concerns and know that we really hear them.

With the development team, I would conduct analysis of the donor population to determine the real effect of field visits on lifetime value. My method of analysis would be similar to that used in the field for program evaluation. Field staff are held to rigorous standards in evaluation—what worked, what didn't, how many interactions, quantifying the impact, and so on. The evaluators will use statistical software to provide precise measurable observations. By framing the impact in the same manner, it shows we take field visits seriously as quantifiable drivers. We are not using anecdotal evidence to persuade staff lacking the luxury of using anecdotes in their own work.

Next, I would reach out to other organizations in the sector to learn how they have tackled the same problems. From your discovery work, you should have some clear directions for your questions. For example, if field workers said they didn't have the time to usher a donor from place to place, how have you managed logistics for donors in the field? Be careful not to let confirmation bias drive your results. The information you gather should not prove it will work for you. Your goal is to gather ideas for potential pathways.

After compiling your analysis, you should be able to outline the key challenges and benefits for both sides and some potential solutions from the other organizations. This is the time to reconvene the task force for a solution brainstorming session. This meeting will not solve all the problems, either. Your goal is to have several ideas for each of the challenge areas.

Following this meeting, you will need to evaluate the cost-benefit of the ideas. Maybe hiring a position in the field to usher donors around would work well, but the cost of the position may not be feasible. Which budget line would fund the position? Might a key board member or donor help fund a donor field experience program? This analysis should result in a pathway of recommendations to test and refine with the task force. The final report should appear as rigorous as a field evaluation report.

After agreeing to a path forward, it is time to assemble the work plan for meeting the recommendations. This will include socializing the plan as well as implementing it. Here is where your fundraising skills get to shine. Obviously, presenting the report to the field is a good start. You might give a web presentation in addition to sending the report. Let's say you discovered a few field workers who really enjoy the donor visits. Additionally, the visits to their location are among the more successful in donor transformation. You could produce a video interviewing them and highlighting their success. This video could be part of your presentation. You may create an internal marketing plan. You could assign fundraisers to specific field workers for personal cultivation. Perhaps you could connect field staff to each other.

The takeaway from this example is effort. Your culture will not change because you hope it will change. But it can change. A fundraising advocate understands that propensity building requires strategy, time, and commitment.

AN ADVOCATE IN THE PUBLIC SPACE

I must admit I'm not much of a fan of politics. I am, however, incredibly passionate about the nonprofit sector and the many selfless donors I see making the world a better place. I have such confidence in nonprofits solving problems. And I feel I am more effective focusing my efforts to the betterment of our sector. As a result, I have left little in the tank to tackle civic engagement.

Philanthropy benefits from fundraisers advocating on its behalf. Advocating is not only on the national stage, it might be in your backyard. (And partisan politics need not apply.) Any time we chose to advance or promote our profession and the good it does for the world, we are doing a good thing.

Have you ever spoken at a career day at a local school? I'm embarrassed to say my daughters have blocked me at every turn. Apparently, I'm not as cool as the guy who works for the Minnesota Vikings or flies for Delta Airlines. But I love my work. Many people I meet love their work. It is fun being out of the office, meeting fascinating people, and doing really important work that has lasting significance. It's an ideal career! If we are going to start to tackle our talent gap, we need to build some understanding with our youth.

I was struck by a finding in the *Giving USA Special Report on Giving to Religion* (Giving USA, October 24, 2017). Most people not working in the religious sector likely ignored the report, but the secular implications might be worth consideration. The report shows people affiliated with religion give more even beyond religious designations in counts and amounts. Among religiously affiliated people, 62% give, whereas 46% of the unaffiliated give. The religious households give $1,590 annually when looking beyond religion, whereas unaffiliated donors give $695. Pew Research Center shows rapid declines in religious affiliation year after year. What impact might this have?

I'm not making an appeal for religious affiliation; that would be a different book. Instead, I want to think about this in the context of advocacy. Religion exposes giving to young people regularly. In Christian circles, there are Sunday School collections, fundraisers for missions, and a weekly passing of the plate. In Jewish circles, philanthropy is taught at a young age. The Jewish Federation has many programs for youth that expose them to giving principles. *Zakat*, a word for *charity*, is the Third Pillar of Islam. Will the declines in religious affiliation correlate with a decline in early exposure to philanthropy?

The closest bright spot I see is checkout charity. When the cashier asks a parent to give a dollar for children or animals, the child witnesses the solicitation. They see if their parent says yes or no. And, they participate in the recognition by writing their name on the heart, clover, or rainbow taped up on the wall behind the register. The value of checkout charity is so much more than that dollar. This is early education and normalization of giving.

In a typical week, I am on an airplane around three times visiting clients, giving talks, or meeting with donors. I am not the most social traveler. I am a quicker draw than Billy the Kid with my ear buds. But I am not an antisocial person. I arrived at this point from this familiar script:

The Traveling Fundraiser

Scene 1.

Josh takes his seat on the plane next to a random stranger on a Friday evening. The flight attendant is making announcements over the PA. Other passengers stream onto the plane, coveting space for their overpacked roller boards.

RANDOM SEATMATE

Good evening.

JOSH

Good evening.

RANDOM SEATMATE

So, are you heading home or heading out?

JOSH

Going home. You?

RANDOM SEATMATE

Yup. Same. Been a long week.

Can't wait to see the kids. Anyway, what
do you do?

*In that moment, all of the conversations that
happened before rushed through Josh's head. Do I say
"fundraising"? "Fundraising consultant"? "Manage a
firm"? Do I lie? Why does this always happen to me?*

JOSH
Consulting. You?

RANDOM SEATMATE
I sell packing materials.
So, what do you consult about?

JOSH
Fundraising.

RANDOM SEATMATE
That's great.
You know, my kid is selling chocolate bars to raise
money for the band program.

JOSH
Yup. It's just like that.

*Josh inserts his earbuds in one fluid motion while
pretending to rest his head for a well-deserved nap.*

SCENE

I know I could handle that scene so much differently.
I have no excuse not to! A *fundraising advocate* would take this
opportunity to explain how wonderful our profession is. He
would explain what a joy it is to meet with fascinating people
and solve the world's biggest problems. He would provide an
anecdote about a kid he met at a children's hospital who
would not be alive without the new treatment that was
funded five years before. He would say he has the best job in
the world.

But, alas, I am part of the problem. I should take advantage of every opportunity to promote fundraising and the joy of giving—so should we all. I want to challenge our profession to go to the career days. Speak at an event outside of our sector. Represent your organization at town halls. And if you have it in you, advocate at a national level. Join a policy committee. Meet your representatives. Tell your story

BE *THAT* PERSON

One of my goals is to be a Larry, Mary, Randy, or Shelby. What an honor it would be to have helped someone achieve career success by believing in them. In a profession defined by encouraging others to give, how can I be a better giver?

I hope you have the same goal. Be that person in someone's bio. Volunteer for one of the many professional associations. Invite that staff member to speak. Bring one of your faculty members or doctors to a conference with you. Teach a nonprofit fundraising class at a local college. Take on some interns from the community. This is what great fundraisers do.

ADVOCACY REQUIRES PASSION

I can't stop talking about fundraising, so much so that it bleeds into other aspects of my life. You could say I have boundary issues.

For me, it is so much more than a profession, it's a lifestyle and lifelong consuming obsession. I love how fundraising connects us to people we would not normally meet. I love how it affects every aspect of an organization. I can't imagine doing anything else with my life, unless it were producing on Broadway, but even that involves investors and raising money. The fundraising advocate is passionate about fundraising. You can read more about this in Chapter 4. But to me, how we advocate is just as important as why we advocate.

MENTORING UP

There have been several influential people in my fundraising career. Let me start by saying I truly have learned incredibly valuable lessons from each one of my previous supervisors or organizational leaders. But perhaps what has been of greater importance were the mentors placed in my path—senior peers who were not my direct supervisors but who took on a mentoring role for me.

My first mentor was Amy, now at Stanford University but who at the time was in charge of individual giving at my first development position in California. She was a former human resources professional who had fallen into fundraising. She showed me the ropes of planning, strategy, and execution for donor groups and all things individual giving. I fell in love with individual giving by watching Amy lead. She was fast, intentional, and passionate, and she took action. She knew how to manage an annual fund program but was also excellent with board members and major donors face-to-face.

My next mentor was Dorothy, a retired executive director who became my contract grant writer while I was director of development at a local education center. She imparted her passion for the homeless, for innovation, and for fixing nonprofits. She realized (prior to cell phones) that one of the biggest barriers to homelessness was being unreachable by phone, so she founded a community voicemail so they might interview and be called back for a job. She started nonprofits and turned them around. She was pulled out of retirement three to four times. Dorothy imparted wisdom of how to manage a team, be innovative, persevere, and stay as long as possible in your current position.

My third mentor was Julie, a senior leader at the healthcare system foundation where I used to work. She taught me everything from navigating tricky hospital dynamics to major gifts, to conducting a feasibility study and launching a major capital campaign. She took me under her wing, and we worked in tandem raising more than $100 million for neurosciences.

All three of these women took the time to invest in me as a junior fundraiser and manager. Each woman I now consider a close friend. I strongly recommend mentors who have a passion for teaching and paving the way for the next generation of development professionals and leaders. I took their advice and expertise and use it to this day.

MENTORING DOWN

It is very important to mentor someone who is coming up in the ranks or is newer in the field. I used to mentor a former employee as she took on roles with increasing responsibility at a local Catholic university. As she propelled in her development operations career, we would periodically touch base for lunch and I would help her navigate the next steps in her career. I have also enjoyed intentionally mentoring those in the Rice University Glasscock School's LINE program. I try to offer advice on various ways to use their talents as a fundraising professional and to expand their view of what fundraising is and can be for their careers. To this day, I am still mentoring Cecily, an incredible young Black woman in our profession, thanks to the LINE program. We recently had a wonderful conversation about what we were learning in our current positions instead of how we were progressing up the career ladder. It is amazing what you learn about yourself as you listen, learn from, and mentor others.

MENTORING ALONGSIDE

One of my favorite types of mentoring is alongside peers in the industry. I have gotten increasingly involved on the board of my Association of Fundraising Professionals (AFP) local chapter and as the immediate past president. The peers I have met through AFP have become some of my dearest friends. We encourage, advocate for, and support each other. They are true leaders at each of their respective nonprofits, and I am so glad to know them. They lend an ear when I'm frustrated or show up in the rain at a speaking engagement about this book. This is my tribe; and I am forever grateful to serve alongside them in our industry.

So, go out there and be brave and find your circle of mentors! They are probably already in your life, but you have to take the time to meet and be open to letting them into your circle of trust. Find a seasoned advancement professional who is willing to share their knowledge, find someone you can invest in and impart your expertise to, and then find your tribe of fundraisers who are willing to support you through thick and thin, both personally and professionally. You need all three types of mentorships in order to continue to be successful in this industry.

Your Advocate

Occasionally in your life, there are special people who come along in your fundraising career to be your advocate. An advocate can also be your mentor, but they go beyond the call of duty. An advocate is your career champion. They believe what is possible for your career and invest in you and your ideas as a development professional. They dream for you and empower you to be the very best development professional you can be. They want you to be successful and as a result, an advocate is someone you can trust. An advocate is someone who believes in you, perhaps far more than you have ever believed in yourself. I am grateful to call my co-author Josh Birkholz an advocate in my career.

When I approached Josh about encouraging him to write a second book, he immediately said, "Great idea! Why don't you write it with me?" I had never written a book before. I conveyed my fears of not being able to complete such a monumental undertaking, to which he said, "You'll be great; it's easy. You just have to start writing."

Advocates are hard to find in our industry, so when you find them, hold on and get ready for the ride. You will never know what's possible until someone believes in you, empowers you, and inspires you to do great things for our industry. In return, you can then empower others and inspire them to be the best they can be.

ADVOCATE FOR OUR INDUSTRY

The Donor Bill of Rights begins with a beautiful opening paragraph reminding us why we are in this business of philanthropy:

> Philanthropy is based on voluntary action for the common good. It is a tradition of giving and sharing that is primary to the quality of life. To assure that philanthropy merits the respect and trust of the general public, and that donors and prospective donors can have full confidence in the not-for-profit organizations and causes they are asked to support, we declare all donors have these rights.

The *Donor Bill of Rights* was adopted in 1993 as a collaborative resource for development professionals by the Association of Fundraising Professionals, Association for Healthcare Philanthropy (AHP), Council for Advancement and Support of Education (CASE), and the Giving Institute: Leading Consultants to Non-Profits.

What I love about *The Donor Bill of Rights* is that it comes from a place of trust and through the avenues of honest and transparent communication with our donors. It also protects the donor and us fundraisers from unethical (and many times unintentional) fundraising practices.

The *AFP Code of Ethical Principles* was originally adopted in 1964 to help fundraisers and board members understand the role of philanthropy within the organizations. I relish reading this text from 1964; it is inspiring and captures the weight and heart of our noble profession:

> Members of AFP are motivated by inner drive to improve the quality of life through the cause they serve. They serve

the ideal of philanthropy, are committed to the preservation and enhancement of volunteerism, and hold stewardship of these concepts as the overriding direction of their professional life. They recognize their responsibility to ensure that needed resources are vigorously and ethically sought and that the intent of the donor is honestly fulfilled. To these ends, AFP members, both individual and business, embrace certain values that they strive to uphold in performing their responsibilities for generating philanthropic support.
—Donor Bill of Rights, copyright AFP, AHP, CASE, Giving Institute 2015. Reprinted with permission from the Association of Fundraising Professionals

I find it rare that fundraisers intentionally choose to be malicious and unethical in their practices; in most cases, I found that fundraisers and nonprofits were not educated on ethical fundraising practices in the first place. I am a proud card-carrying member of AFP and keep the card on my desk for a reason. I have been known to use it as a prop with my staff or colleagues to say if I were to do or allow that [insert unethical practice], then I would have to give back my fundraising card.

ADVOCATE WITHIN YOUR ORGANIZATION

I have previously distributed *The Donor Bill of Rights* and *AFP Code of Ethical Standards* to colleagues on my senior management team. I requested they educate themselves on what makes a great fundraiser and asked them to hold me and my organization accountable to these practices. Once we educate our staff, ourselves, and our peers at our organizations, we advance the industry and in turn make our jobs easier. The only way we can stop being frustrated that our colleagues and donors "don't know what I do" or "don't know what fundraising means" is to educate them. Have a mission moment about what fundraising is and how they can help in your staff meetings. Remind your team of our noble profession and how important it is to uphold these professional standards. Ask your team's advice on what practices and processes we should implement in our daily operations to uphold these standards for ourselves and for our donors. Create a culture of philanthropy among your peers by including them in the cultivation or stewardship process so they can better understand what you do. This will lead to greater respect, understanding, and admiration of the professional. I have found that many senior leaders want to understand how they can help with fundraising, as it is a valuable skill set they can use to advance their careers. To not be intimidated talking with a board member or learning how to solicit funds is an incredibly transferable skill set that any professional can take with them in their career. By including your colleagues in the cultivation process, you are also stewarding your donors in a better way by exposing them to other leaders in your organization, thus creating buy-in and trust in the entire leadership team. You can also give these team members portfolios to help track their cultivation or stewardship efforts. As long as you can coordinate these activities and know when to make the ask, all is well. The more you educate and include others in the process, the more you create allies for philanthropy within your organization.

COMMUNITY RELATIONS

I had to teach myself what community relations means related to fundraising. I often joked with my director of marketing colleague that the community relations team was the wall between our adjacent offices. In my most recent role as director of development, I found myself as a point person for community-related events and needs when others were not available. I worked with city council members to make sure they were invited to events. I worked with my team to make sure we got the proclamations necessary for important milestones or that the right people were present at city council meetings to receive the proclamations. I worked with the mayor's office to connect our artistic team so cast members could perform in the city's Thanksgiving Day parade. I worked with a building manager so our name could appear in lights on a nearby office building. I attended our state's Arts Advocacy Day and went strategically door to door talking to our state senators and congresspersons and their staffers about the importance of arts funding. I have worked with a consultant to submit several federal grants for building and education programs and crafted a day for a managing director to meet senators and congresspersons in Washington, D.C. If it fell outside the scope of marketing and operations, many times development spearheads government relations efforts for the organization.

VOLUNTEER ADVOCATE

I highly recommend joining a professional organization or two to round out your networks beyond your organization. Too often we get tied up in the office and do not go out in the community where the connections happen. By joining your local AFP chapter, AHP, CASE, Apra (Association of Professional Researchers for Advancement), aasp (Association of Advancement Services Professionals), or other entities related to your particular sector such as Opera America, National

Alliance for Musical Theatre, League of Resident Theatres, League of American Orchestras, or Tessitura Network, you expand your fundraising and nonprofit networks in a meaningful way.

In addition, you need to add local business entities or chambers to your network. I have joined chamber-type groups, one that was downtown business–focused and another that was women in business–focused. I joined a group for women in the sports industry (WISE) and was thrilled to find the commonalities I had with these ladies in another entertainment industry. By expanding my circle beyond nonprofit fundraising or a sector-specific group, you meet business leaders and potential corporate partners or funders. The larger your network, the more people in your industry and in business will learn about the organization you are representing.

If you have time, I also encourage you to join a nonprofit board or advisory board for an organization or cause that you are passionate about. Nothing allows you to relate more to your own board members than to be on a board yourself.

TEACHING AND SPEAKING

Public speaking has never been a struggle for me since I was a formally trained actor. If it is a struggle for you, I highly recommend taking an adult acting class or course at your local theater or college. Not only will you learn how to project and find your voice, but you learn body awareness, movement, memorization skills, empathy, trust, and collaboration.

I strongly encourage speaking for an online class or webinar if you have the chance. They can be a lot of fun and expose you to participants and nonprofit professionals across the world. I highly recommend guest lecturing virtually or in person at your local universities as well. I have done this several times and really enjoy sparking that passion for nonprofits, fundraising, or analytics with inquiring and inspiring young minds. I'm a lecturer for two online classes at Rice University for the Glasscock School for Continuing Studies, one on Donor Relations and another on Fundraising Analytics. When I started teaching online, it was very hard to gauge the interest of the participants. It's hard to not have that instant feedback or connection. Was I being well received? Did they even like my presentation?

I love speaking at conferences because there is something about the energy of networking at a conference, the fresh and new ideas that is thrilling to me. Even if you don't like conferences, I still encourage you to find an opportunity to speak at a conference session. I joined and co-chaired the development sessions for the Planning Committee of Tessitura Network's conference and enjoyed not only working on a project with others in the industry, but also planning holistic and useful content for other development professionals. Conferences always need good speakers, so if you feel comfortable doing so and have a great topic, please put your hat in the ring. It is great practice, and you can quickly become a resource on a particular topic. Most importantly, conferences get us all in the same room to advance our industry together.

In closing, advocate for yourself, empower others, and find a mentor or be the mentor others have been to you. Together we can all advocate for each other and our industry, creating a better world for our fellow fundraisers, for our organizations, and for those we serve.

CHAPTER DISCUSSION GUIDE

- Name three people you can ask to be your mentor, to be their mentor, or to walk alongside you as a peer. Space is included below to write their names as a reminder:

  1.

  2.

  3.

- How might you be a fundraising advocate for a colleague or staff member?

- What professional organizations can you join to help further your career or your organization?

- Find a fundraising project you are excited about. What conferences or speaking engagements can you participate in to tell the story about your project?

7

THE DIGITAL FACTOR

We need to stop interrupting what people are interested in and be what people are interested in.

—Craig Davis

Much of this book was written before the COVID-19 disruption of 2020. Only one of the concepts substantively changed because of the pandemic. Digital fundraising, while growing rapidly for building the base of support for organizations, became an enterprise-level reality. It was no longer sufficient to have digital fundraising. Fundraising had to become digital.

Leading up to 2020, fundraising in the digital channels lived primarily with the direct response or annual giving teams. Nonprofits solicited gifts over email or on social media.

But major gifts were rarely considered digital fundraising. Remote events were novelties. Zoom calls maybe happened with consultants, but with donors?

In 2021 forward, the new reality confirmed that digital is here to stay. Digital hasn't only helped fundraising adapt to distancing, digital has made fundraising better.

In our analysis, we have found that direct response by traditional channels declines as wealth increases. For this analysis, we had to control for age. As people age, they tend to accumulate wealth. But, within age brackets, wealth had an inverse correlation. We have not observed this same difference in the digital space. As it turns out, very wealthy grandparents also like to view their grandkids pictures on Facebook. Very wealthy people pay attention to Giving Days. Very wealthy people give in response to digital campaigns. And very wealthy people adapted to Zoom, very well.

Another curious behavioral characteristic is when attention happens. Several years ago, I set up my first E-Trade account. I was familiar with the online training site because of the television commercials with the talking babies. I had never been to the website. Eventually, I set up my new account and invested in a few index funds. Intellectually, I know that investments of this type are long-game investments. Nevertheless, I think I checked out my funds on the E-Trade site about 15 times that first week. After I made my first substantial transaction, I wanted to know how they were performing.

Soon after donors make major gifts, they tend to check out the website and social channels. Perhaps it is from a sense of validating their choices. Maybe they just feel really great at those moments and want to check on their philanthropic investments. Either way, we have their attention.

We know potential major donors live in the digital space. We know potential major donors pay attention to the digital space. We know potential major donors give in the digital space. We know major donors check back on their previous investments. How might we leverage the digital space to cultivate major gifts? I would suggest we have many potential options, but I want to elaborate on content framing, prospecting, warming, cultivation, and donor relations.

CONTENT FRAMING

In Chapter 5, I described organizational esteem. Elite charities seem to have an easier time asking for big gifts because they are the types of charities that get big gifts. This is ultimately a branding question. Some charities have effective brands for the high-net-worth marketplace.

For your digital content to align in the high-net-worth community, you need to define the population, go where they are, and use language that resonates with them. Seth Godin described the smallest viable audience concept in his book *This Is Marketing* (Portfolio Penguin, 2018). He said, "The smallest viable audience approach means figuring out who the people are who care enough about what you're selling to get in their car and drive five miles, or twenty miles, instead of walking across the street to buy something average—and committing yourself to focusing just on them." Most of the digital marketing I see at nonprofits is focused on a very large audience of donors of all sizes, with little concerted focus on the donors giving the biggest sums.

After evaluating digital marketing content for charities closing the biggest gifts, I formulated my ideas into a concept called *The Impact Maturity Model* (BWF, 2017). It outlines four stages of maturity in communicating in a way that resonates with a donor population.

STAGE 1. INTERNAL NEED-BASED

Emerging and less successful charities will make the case for giving by indicating they need the money. Typically, people who are new to fundraising or unfamiliar with philanthropic motivations think if you tell people you need help, they will help you. Some good examples are church bulletins showing a failure to meet budget with the hopes people will make up the gap, teachers making the case for elementary school supplies, and Wikipedia's push for funds. Here is Wikipedia's 2019 appeal.

> *To all our readers in the U.S., It's a little awkward, so we'll get straight to the point: This Saturday we humbly ask you to defend Wikipedia's independence. We depend on donations averaging about $16.36, but 98% of our readers don't give. If everyone reading this gave $2.75, we could keep Wikipedia thriving for years to come. The price of your Saturday coffee is all we need. The heart and soul of Wikipedia is a community of people working to bring you unlimited access to reliable, neutral information. We know that most people will ignore this message. But if Wikipedia is useful to you, please take a minute to help keep it growing. Thank you.*

If giving a major gift is truly closer to investing, think about what message this sends. Also, guilt is not an effective long-term, sustainable motivator. Imagine a public company saying, "We are having a really challenging year. Our earnings are not what they used to be. We are not sure if we need to lay off employees or close some branches. Now, more than ever, we need you to invest in our stock." Would you make that investment? Surely not. We invest because we want a return. If that return is a better world off on the horizon, we'd rather get on the fastest boat than start fixing the broken one.

STAGE 2. EXTERNAL NEED-BASED

Over time, charities will begin to externalize their needs. Rather than saying, "We need your help," they will say, "The people or causes we serve need your help." This is the zone of sick and injured animals in cages with guilt messaging and sappy soundtracks. These pity-eliciting appeals are commonly called, "pity porn." It's an unfortunate name. But it is an even more unfortunate tactic.

Occasionally, people will be overcome with guilt and give. But, organizations with externalized need-based messaging will struggle with retention. Giving should be fun, rewarding, and enlightening. Just the act of going to one of these sites is a major downer. The experience is not one of achieving elation. It is one of alleviating discomfort. There are easier ways to avoid discomfort. The most common way is to walk away.

STAGE 3. INTERNAL IMPACT-BASED

Now we are maturing to a stage that begins to resonate with donors. Rather than focus on the problems, we focus on our successful history and practice of problem solving. Impact messages are forward looking, grounded in success, and offer hope. Sometimes, however, they can leave the donors out of the equation.

Internal impact-based messaging focuses on how the organization solves all the world's problems. It checks all the boxes for a good investment. But it misses out on an intimate relationship with the donors and the personal satisfaction they seek. We require the donor to make the connection that *I can have impact by giving to you, who will then do the good stuff.*

STAGE 4. EXTERNAL IMPACT

The most effective content framing to high-wealth audiences and to our closest donors is to give them the credit for the impact. Rather than focus on the many scholarships your university offers, talk about the first-generation student who went on to do great things because Sally Donor funded his journey. Rather than describing the land you are conserving, point out how Steve Benefactor felt future generations would benefit from his selfless gift of land. You are the one speaking. Donors realize you did the work.

If we are trying to connect with the smallest viable high net worth audience, think about how powerful a catered external impact message can be. Let's say you received your first commitment from one of the Giving Pledge donors named Philip Anthropy. Maybe this gift will feed thousands of kids per year. Providing video content to Phil's closest friends and your other high-net-worth prospects showing how *Phil* is helping all these will outperform a video showing how your organization is helping all these kids.

Even stronger than helping thousands of kids, I would point out one kid. Nobel Prize–winning economist, Richard Thaler, points out that we value the identified individual more than we value the statistical individual. We value research that saves the life of little Emily Smith more than we value research that saves thousands of little children.

Framing your content in the digital space requires defining your smallest viable audience, providing impact-based messaging around your case and priorities, including the donor role in the equation, and relating the message to identified recipients.

PROSPECTING

Facebook is a platform for marketing to audiences with very specific criteria. The volume of data Facebook has on each individual is incredible. They have more accurate wealth data than all the screening companies, and their assortment of interests is incredibly precise. Fortunately, they do not let people just buy this data from them. Instead, they let you define the population so that you can market to them. If they engage with you, then you can know who the constituent is.

In recent years, people have become gun-shy about using Facebook because of recent abuses. A few bad actors in the political sphere realized you could buy lots of ads on many defined profiles. Let's say an outfit wanted to determine if people had some characteristic they were unwilling to share. For this example, let's say preferring dogs over cats was somehow controversial. They might send one ad to an anonymous population of people who like dogs and send another ad to people who like cats. The ads had nothing to do with cats or dogs. It might have been a fun quiz like which of these foods could you live without. If they could trick the person into clicking on the ad, they could identify if the person was in the dog group or cat group based on which ad they clicked into. Then, they could farm the data into a database. These bait-and-switch tactics were unethical and certainly caused a storm.

However, because some folks were unethical and made poor choices does not mean there aren't very ethical ways to market in the Facebook universe. Let's say your university planned to build the first International Museum of Badminton. For some reason, you have an amazing collection of badminton memorabilia. And, you have a few donors who are very interested. This would be the type of project that does not test well in feasibility studies. No consultant would likely say, "Go for it. That sounds like a winner!" You may be thinking the project is a nonstarter.

This would be the type of project that could benefit from digital prospecting. I would start by producing some key content pieces. Perhaps the first is a video about the exciting new center. Maybe the second piece is a case outline of sorts. Maybe the third is a piece about a specific badminton donor. Next, I would buy access to people with major gift assets and have a passion for badminton and place the ads to their pages.

When your prospects click on a page, your landing page will appear, which has a remarketing cookie, and it will fire a tracking pixel. This will indicate that the next ad the prospects see is the second piece of content. If they continue to engage in your content, you can send the name to the prospect research office for verification. You will have names of people who have the capacity to give, have a defined interest in your cause, and have also engaged in your content. Reaching out to them for a discovery interaction will not seem inappropriate to them. You are connecting with them over something they want.

The key to ethical prospecting in the digital space is relevance and donor-driven initiation. The content must be relevant to the recipient. And, the recipient should initiate engagement by interacting with your content.

WARMING

In several parts of this book, we discussed the challenges of discovery work. Making the first contact with a prospective donor is often the most uncomfortable step for most officers. The main complaint from the discovery officer is how cold the relationship was. Certainly, the transition from one-to-many fundraising to one-to-one fundraising is a challenging shift. My team has seen some success in assisting this transition by incorporating digital warming.

Prospecting in the digital space requires engaging people you do not know. Warming in the digital space requires engaging people you do know. If you have a mature prospect development team, you likely have more prospects than you know what to do with. At least, you probably have many prospects with capacity and propensity, regardless of whether anyone has actually met them.

There are ways to load this population into social platforms for targeted ad placement. You could place videos about the upcoming campaign. Perhaps you could provide some impact videos. You may even place simple ads about when people give to you. If the donor engages in the content, you may be able to make first contact with them right there in the digital space. You could begin chatting with them or set up a quick zoom call. If you connect with a prospective donor using other channels, you may benefit from a warming lift. They may think, I don't know why I've been thinking about you, but I have been lately. The warming doesn't do the discovery work for you, but it helps to clear the path.

You may pair this warming with a direct marketing approach for discovery. I've seen success in using targeted discovery mailings and outsourced discovery calling, following initial warming treatment. As with prospecting, the messaging must be relevant to the donor and transparent in its objective.

CULTIVATION

My colleague, Justin Ware, founder of Groundwork Digital, a BWF Company, and co-founder of {{firstname}}, an enterprise-wide digital fundraising company, has trained digital development officers for many organizations over the past few years. Some donors respond very well to interacting first in the digital environment. Across his clients, he has seen many examples of major gifts being closed entirely in the digital space. Here are some of the steps he uses in the programs he builds:

1. Develop video-driven donor engagement strategies.
2. Use automation strategies to target donors with personalized content that helps the message stand out from other nonprofits.
3. Train the officers in using the digital tools with confidence so they can stay front and center with the donors on a daily basis and cultivate them with mission and gift opportunities.
4. Set up microsites for individual donors.

5. Create digital action plans customized to each officer.

6. Incorporate corresponding stewardship strategies in the digital space.

A very common challenge I see at many organizations is online messaging and web content failing to align with major gift messaging. Most fundraisers are attuned to impact-based messaging and philanthropic priorities. Sometimes, it looks like the digital marketers never talked to the major gift team. As with my E-Trade example in the earlier content framing section, we know donors will check out the website and the social channels when they give. When they change the channel, do they see the same program?

Even if you do not raise gifts online, I would suggest working hard to see that your messages align for the major donors. Although I am a believer that you can raise gifts online, even having complementary content will provide value in the cultivation process.

Giving Days are very popular whether they are Giving Tuesday events, region-specific events, or institution-based events. Most organizations use these days as a base development strategy. There is also a major gift benefit to Giving Days.

In our source and journey analysis projects, we have discovered that the entry channel of major donors is shifting. For many organizations, the first gift a major donor ever gave was a direct mail gift. People still give lots of gifts through the mail. But the donors who start giving through the mail and become major donors later are declining rapidly. The phone, still a very effective midrange, pathway and renewal channel, is also declining in its sourcing of future major gift donors. The areas that are taking its place are peer-to-peer (whether in person or online) and events.

A Giving Day is one of the most effective tools to begin a donor journey for a future major donor. This is especially the case when the Giving Day incorporates peer ambassadors. The strength of another donor making a gift and inviting others to participate taps into that peer-to-peer preference.

The other benefit of Giving Days for major giving is the marketing benefit. We've found that major donors, regardless of donating to the Giving Day, pay attention to the content throughout the day. They are excited to see other constituents support the organization they hold dearly. This is a great opportunity to solicit a gift match or a testimonial video.

Another strategy for countering the declines in traditional base development channels is the student engagement team. Some of the early-use cases have outperformed traditional phone programs. To date, these are mainly emerging in the education sector. But, the concept could be easily transferable to other junior staff members. I asked my colleague Justin Ware to outline how these programs work. He says:

> Student engagement teams are proven donor engagement programs that connect key constituencies to an organization. These programs help strengthen donors' interest in supporting an organization by creating a consistent and ongoing stream of content that reinforces their decision to give while also attracting new donors with dynamic content delivered on a more frequent basis.
>
> We start by hiring, training, and deploying the teams—from content production to online constituent engagement. We build volunteers and students into effective "Digital

Development Officers." These teams will have a video producer (generally outsourced) working with the engagement team members to guarantee they have compelling content to share with donors and prospects. Engagement teams support multi-channel campaigns, elevate digital campaigns such as giving days, and cultivate and steward leadership annual and major gift donors and prospects.

The teams are made up of qualified students at a college or university (paid positions, like student callers) or top volunteers at a nonprofit who are chosen to participate. Development staff members will need to approve the video strategy, campaign plans, and copy.

As a result, the fully functioning, trained, and dedicated content team will provide videos that are ready to deploy for immediate engagement. This dynamic content is both fresh and authentic and can engage every level of an organization's donors and prospects.

DONOR RELATIONS

Throughout the chapter, I've tried to make the case that donors pay attention to the digital space, and even more so after they become engaged. This makes the online environment a perfect setting for donor relations.

With several clients, we have surveyed both the donors and the fundraisers to understand their alignment. One question that continues to show separation is, "What do you most value from the development department?" Or, when asked of fundraisers, "What is the most valuable thing development offers to the donors?" For the donors, "How my gifts are used" is the top or among the top three in nearly every survey. "How a donor's gifts are used" rarely breaks the top three in the fundraiser surveys.

The donor experience is the most valued and also most underinvested strategy in many development programs. Organizations will spend top dollar to build the base, identify major gift prospects, cultivate major gifts, and support this process with technology. But dedicated professionals to the donor relations is relatively sparse and mainly carried by one or a handful of dedicated professionals. What is it like to be a donor to your organization? Is this a question you ask often enough in staff meetings? How often is donor experience management an area of innovation in your strategic plan?

I would start by valuing and staffing donor relations the way it should be staffed. Part of this investment should be in the digital space. Video content is inexpensive, and the channel is cheap. You could create a simple video about a campaign priority. Then you could invite program staff, faculty, individual fundraisers, or your leadership to provide bookends to the video. The script is rather straightforward. Here is an example.

Opening bookend
CARE CENTER REPRESENTATIVE
Hi Josh and Tracy.
I just wanted to let you know how much we appreciate your support for our new memory center.
I thought you'd like to see how the building project is coming along.
Cut to the memory center video.
Video plays
Cut back to closing bookend
CARE CENTER REPRESENTATIVE
We are just so thrilled you share our passion for providing dignity of care to people with dementia.

> Next time you are in our area, bring your girls and
> we'll give you a tour of the facility. We appreciate
> you more than you know.

This bookend would take no more than a couple of minutes of a representative of the nonprofit. The impact to the donor is great. With the state of video technology today, you can create really exceptional content with fractions of the budget you might expect.

Another way of leveraging digital technology for donor relations is to gather content from your field staff, doctors, actors, faculty, or researchers. Share papers they wrote based on funded research. Share news items or upcoming events. The key with major donors is to personalize the content. Share it with them by direct message or text. Give them an opportunity to engage with questions. Perhaps the staff does not have time to engage, but you can be their voice. Your digital donor relations officer can also keep the conversation going.

The ultimate goal is to maintain momentum—especially over multiyear pledges. When you make the shift back to cultivating them for the next gift, it will feel natural to continue the conversation.

SEA CHANGE

In 2018, Eric Kinariwala said 7,000 brick-and-mortar stores closed by the end of 2017. He went on to say, "Storefronts aren't folding because people are buying less—they're doing so because people are buying differently" ("The Third Wave of Digital Commerce," *Forbes*, May 2018).

The trend of commerce shifting to the digital space is not news to anyone, especially following the 2020 pandemic.

But the shift is also happening in high-touch fields like service. When Amazon launched its Geek Squad competitor in technical support, Best Buy saw a loss of $1 billion in value. Stockholders saw the writing on the wall.

In my 2018 paper, "Platform Fundraising Is Here. Are You Truly Ready for It?," I closed with the following statement, which seems quite fitting for this chapter.

> It is time for innovation to once again dethrone best practices. If we maintain a conformity to common methods, we will miss out on this truly defining moment for our profession. Digital, social, online, interactive, etc. are not tools in the tool belt, they are the early signals of a massive sea change. Let's embrace that change. Our numbers won't decline because people are giving less—they will do so because people are giving differently.

FUNDRAISING IN A TECHNOLOGY INTEGRATED ERA

I am a member of the advisory board of a small nonprofit that provides water wells and radios to South Sudan. I received the most amazing and personalized video from the executive director who said my name and thanked me for the impact of my gift as he was riding in the back of a jeep through the trees in South Sudan. That moment made me feel like I was there in the action. I have never been to South Sudan, but in one effective virtual moment he made me feel that my gift made a difference. Donors no longer have to travel to places like Africa to see the impact of their gifts. We can now experience video content that connects us directly to the beneficiaries of our generosity.

During the pandemic, US e-commerce penetration fast forwarded by a full decade according to a McKinsey study. However, well before the pandemic, donors were engaging with their nonprofits in the digital space through avenues like online giving and social media. We as fundraisers are now becoming more well versed on how to take this new digital culture and overlay it on everything we do and how we communicate. We have gone beyond making that social-media-savvy staff member in the office do digital work for the organization. Digital is now everyone's business and especially the fundraisers. Social media carries robust tools that, if partnered with your marketing team, can leverage the entire donor experience from a modern, multichannel perspective.

That is what the digital space does well. It meets our donors online wherever they are, whether it is on social media watching their grandchildren's adventures or posting vacation pictures with their families. My cultivation strategies with major donors and board members in the social space have now begun to mimic those interactions with friends and family who I do not see that often due to the pandemic.

We have had to adapt to using all communication mediums in our personal lives, so why not communicate with our donors in the same way. We text to meet at their homes, we comment and like each other's social media posts, we email to set up a dinner, we deepen the relationship in person, but we find ourselves communicating digitally to get the logistics out of the way. Digital communication can enhance the relationship between the times when you see each other again in person, but it will never completely suffice for face-to-face relationship building, communication and interaction. Digital can get you in the literal living rooms for the deep meaningful cultivation to happen. And if you are not able to get to the physical living room, digital effectively helps you meet virtually through Zoom or Teams.

We have become a more insular society, for better or worse, thereby replacing many large social gatherings with keeping up with acquaintances and distant family and friends through online voyeurism. Therefore, we as fundraisers have to adapt to this new digital connectivity through innovative digital techniques such as lead-generation campaigns, digital warming, the digital donor journey, and multichannel fundraising. We must think well beyond the virtual event and how we handle moves management and mass donor communication entirely from the digital space.

DIGITAL DISRUPTION

Digital disruption occurs when new digital technologies and business models affect how we do business and deliver goods and services. Think streaming services, the long extinction of the local video store chain, curbside pick-up at grocery stores, e-cards, and online shopping. Nonprofit organizations and their fundraisers must embrace digital disruption to stay competitive in a changing philanthropic landscape. Our fundraising business has especially been disrupted as a result of the pandemic and will continue to change with the digital age.

Two particular technologies that have forever disrupted our digital fundraising space are the smart phone and social media. In June of 2007, Apple forever changed the way people used their smart phones with the release of the iPhone combining technologies of music, phone, camera, and Internet connection. The invention of a sleek patented touch screen now allowed users to carry their laptop communication functionality with them every day. As the smart phone screen has increased in size, so has the dependency on using it for everyday work. The gift officer's office has become more mobile, with gift officers having hotel space and using laptops for business, but relying on their phones to communicate between projects. I remember seeing a talk by an education futurist in 2009 about how the office four walls would no longer exist as employees will be able to work anywhere and everywhere. I thought this was a crazy concept at the time, but this has now become particularly true with hybrid work environments as a result of the pandemic.

"Senior citizens in the US are the fastest growing group of Facebook users nearly doubling in numbers between 2012 and 2019, a vast shift from the platform's beginnings as a service for college students" ("US Facebook Users Are Getting Older," Quartz Media, Inc., published September 11, 2019; updated April 2, 2020). This means that for those of us for whom donor bases are primarily in the baby-boomer age and older, social media is where we can also meet them digitally to tell our stories. I look at how my mom and dad interact with their smartphones. They are using them on a regular basis to text in large print, send pictures, and check their friends and family posts on social media. Our parents may not know all the social media etiquette, but are very active users.

COMMUNICATION AND CONNECTIVITY IN THE DIGITAL AGE

I heard the great Penelope Burk speak once at AFP ICON about how communication has drastically changed since she began her surveys decades ago. Back then, donors who were surveyed preferred several-page newsletters, then eventually over time her survey found that they started to request three to four pages to read, then eventually they requested one page, now they want to read anything they can view from their smart phone screen.

With the distractions all around us and our attention span shortening, that is why it is even more critical than ever to tell our organization's story, quickly and effectively, and, where possible, use video. You can expect someone to spend three to five minutes reading an article or letter before they move on. That's why I am a big proponent of creating one-pagers to convey donor information. A donor will not read past more than a one- to two-page letter, nor will they have time to read your entire newsletter or 30-page annual report. I personally really like the reading times on news articles, so I know whether I have time to read it at the moment or not. I recommend we as fundraisers start using reading times on our newsletters or articles to donors. Maybe it will help with open rates.

In a disconnected society, it is critical more than ever to create meaningful connections with our donors. It is commonly known in marketing that it takes 7–12 connections for a consumer to take action on product or experience. Similarly, we should expect at least seven interactions for a donor to make a gift with an organization. Therefore, we as fundraisers must work in tandem with our marketing teams to create these digital engagement opportunities so donors are primed for the eventual face-to-face cultivation. We are dealing with information overload and message saturation. So how do we as fundraisers combat this message saturation and overload? With great images, videos, and stories. Our email campaigns have to be even more targeted and segmented to reach the user amidst all the other emails they now receive. Marketing and fundraising must work hand-in-hand to produce digital content that is engaging and easy for donors to quickly read and consume.

At a theater I worked at previously, I implemented a text fundraising campaign with the use of strategic texts related to video content and then a soft ask at year-end. Texting was an incredibly effective way to communicate with patrons but must be used with caution. It also proved to be very effective in an emergency when the theater flooded after a hurricane and there was not a way of collecting online funds to help with relief efforts because the servers were down. With this text-to-give software, the theater was able to mobilize quickly and receive online donations in their greatest time of need. I have also seen them used as donation forms at events and performances.

STORYTELLING IN THE DIGITAL AGE

Digital technology allows us a much larger scope to tell stories that were pretty much the grounds of the literary media.
—George Lucas

At the end of the day, we as humans want to connect with other humans through the medium of storytelling. Since the prehistoric era, humans have been telling stories to their communities even before words were invented. William Shakespeare's plays during the Elizabethan era were so widely received not just because their iambic pentamer rhythm mimicked the heartbeat but also because his stories appealed to the masses—the educated aristocrats as well as the groundlings who were largely not literate. Now in the digital era, we as humans always appreciate a good story told in new digital mediums, so as fundraisers we must use this to our advantage. Videos have a unique opportunity to tell a powerful story to a donor in under two minutes.

MULTICHANNEL FUNDRAISING

Early in my career, I once drove three hours west from Houston to San Antonio just to see the fundraising direct mail legend Mal Warwick speak at a local AFP conference. As a young and eager fundraiser, I was very excited to meet Mal as he shared key insights of what worked and didn't in a direct mail campaign. Twenty years ago, Mal Warwick was using his marketing expertise and passion for advocacy, nonprofits, and social justice to change the face of how fundraisers implemented direct mail campaigns. He was the Bernie Sanders of nonprofits giving us the tools to fight the advertisers on Wall Street so our organizations could be heard from the mailboxes.

I like to watch key innovators in our space to see how they chart the territory. What this leads me to believe about digital fundraising is when innovators (like Mal and Josh) focus their consulting efforts on digital, we as fundraisers should all take notice. This is where our fundraising trends are currently and where they are heading. Digital will continue to be a key part of our fundraising efforts. Do we abandon the paper direct mail? Of course not! I have noticed in my own personal mailbox, especially during the pandemic, a decrease in direct mail from advertisers, which means your year-end appeal (if captivating and eye-catching) now has a far greater likelihood of being opened and read.

DIGITAL DONOR JOURNEY

When I first learned about the digital donor journey from my colleagues at {{firstname}}, it was as though a light bulb went off for me as a giving professional. Let's learn from them what the digital donor journey is:

> When we talk about donor journeys, we are really talking about all the steps it takes to go from being a prospective donor to making a gift. We want to put ourselves in our audience's seat, focus on the donor experience, to stay top of mind. An easy way to think about this is in stages of the donor's experience or the donor's journey. Giving Days are a great time to test out these campaigns, because we have a very clear date we are working towards, and a few other factors working in our favor, like urgency and focused attention. The ultimate goal is to have our audience primed and ready to make a gift because of all the work we put in beforehand. We want warm audiences, so we can avoid making cold asks.

Usually when I start working with a client on their digital fundraising content and delivery, we go through the framework of the five stages of the digital donor journey: *Awareness, Consideration, Intent, Conversion and Stewardship.* We look at their multichannel campaign or Giving Day through these five stages and are able to map out communications that follow this structure. These stages act as a roadmap to give intention and purpose to the journey and offer a cadence to digital communications.

CULTIVATING DIFFERENT GENERATIONS

As a Gen Xer, I did not grow up with computers, but one of my earliest memories was playing old-school Oregon Trail in the elementary school library. I fought hard to not have a cell phone in college but eventually gave in post-graduation. I have adapted to the changes in our digital technology and now cannot imagine living without my phone, which is a problem. Unlike me, Gen Y and Z grew up with technology, so they have been the first adopters of how to integrate technology in their social circles. I remember when my youngest millennial brother was introduced to his college roommates through this new tool called Facebook. Now, as an adult in his spare time, he is successfully using video content to engage tens of thousands of Twitter followers around a major league sports team. When communicating digitally with my generation and those younger, I think it's important to remember that again—no matter our age—we all crave one-on-one experiences and interactions. You can easily start with a digital cultivation campaign, but think about how to translate that work into a special or unique in-person experience. Our work in relationship building as development professionals is always cemented by in-person connections.

A media outlet approached me last year asking how millennials are interacting as philanthropists in the digital age, and my answer was engagement. Millennials want to be a part of the solution as volunteers and advocates and not just as donors. I think millennials and Gen Z have gotten an incredibly bad rap in the past because older generations did (and do) not understand them, but we all have a lot to learn from how they interact in the digital space. If you want to up your digital fundraising game, ask socially savvy millennial colleagues how they would integrate your next campaign in the digital space. They will be an invaluable resource on effective modern multichannel communication. And amidst the Great Resignation, millennials are not only our future leaders in the sector they also will be taking the helms as executive directors by their sheer numbers. Gen Xers are not able to fill all the empty leadership roles the baby boomers are leaving behind. We must empower the Gen Y and Z development professionals today to be the fundraising leaders of tomorrow.

CHAPTER DISCUSSION GUIDE

- How can you better integrate current donor cultivation strategies into the digital space?
- What are some multichannel efforts you can start instituting in your direct mail appeals?
- What video content could help enhance your fundraising efforts?
- How can digital storytelling play a bigger role in how you communicate your mission?
- How do you or can you adapt your fundraising programs to Gen Y and Z audiences?

8

THE LEADERSHIP FACTOR

Wealth is not new. Neither is charity. But the idea of using private wealth imaginatively, constructively, and systematically to attack the fundamental problems of mankind is new.

—John Gardner

If your actions inspire others to dream more, learn more, do more and become more, you are a leader.

—John Quincy Adams

Fundraising is not a new concept. There are examples of people contributing to a building fund in ancient times. Around the world, people have asked for money to help others since recorded history began. The National Philanthropic Trust has a fascinating history of modern fundraising at historyofgiving.org. If you visit the site, you will see that they lead with the same John Gardner quote above. In this short statement is the essence of the biggest change to happen to our field. Although fundraising is not new, the *business* of fundraising really emerged during our lifetimes.

I remember a conversation I had about a decade ago with Jerry May, the very successful and long-serving university fundraiser most associated with the University of Michigan and The Ohio State University. We were talking about his early years of leadership versus his later years. To my best recollection, he said, "When I was starting, my focus was on building relationships with my board, finding a way of working well with the president, and strategizing about million dollar asks. After several decades, I've become close friends with many board members. I have a good rapport with the president. And I've closed nine figure gifts. But, I'm not sure I was fully prepared to manage a team of 600 people." The honesty and wisdom of that sentiment has stuck with me.

Until recently, the chief development officer for most charities was the most effective frontline fundraiser who had climbed the ranks as the organization grew. Beginning most noticeably in the 1970s, fundraising started to take on a distributed business model. Rather than single contributors doing all the work, we began to distribute tasks like a business. We had an advancement-services professional manage our records and gifts, the first prospect researchers emerged, we started to see annual-giving professionals and planned-giving professionals, and we had very business-like roles such as marketing, HR, and information technology housed within the development program.

Over the next few decades, programs grew in line with a campaign arms race. The fundraising campaign moved from the incremental capital effort or special initiative to the all-encompassing organizational branding and transformation effort. Along with other businesses, we embraced strategic planning, moved to relational customer relationship management (CRM) databases, incorporated data science, developed digital strategies, established mission and vision language, conducted multiyear plans, created proactive talent management and recruiting strategies, and built a multifaceted professional association ecosystem. Fundraising became a legitimate business.

Now, we are in a period of professionals moving into leadership roles who "grew up" in the business of fundraising. These are different types of leaders with new challenges and opportunities. At times I fear the gradual extinction of the elite fundraiser who honed her craft with top donors over the years only to be replaced with business strategists. But these concepts are not mutually exclusive. Great fundraising leaders continue to emerge. The craft of fundraising continues to evolve.

The characteristics that define a great fundraising leader in the 21st century are being driven by character, being a student of the business, embracing fundamentals, pursuing the edge, and modeling excellence for the organization. As with all areas of fundraising, excellence emerges from a commitment to craft. All of these elements are achievable through commitment and practice. Let's jump in.

Driven by Character

In Chapter 2, I introduced you to my friend and mentor, Fred Kiel. I was honored to provide some assistance in the empirical research for his book *Return on Character*—the next book you should read after this one. This analysis dug into the universal character traits of forgiveness, integrity, compassion, and responsibility. All cultures, regardless of religious or historic backgrounds, have these traits. Through deep analysis of business leaders across sectors—public, private, for profit, and nonprofit—including personal evaluation and employee observation, the team ranked each executive on a character curve. At the top of the curve were virtuosos of character, demonstrating behaviors consistent with all four of the character traits. At the bottom of the curve were some very interesting executives dominated by self-focus.

The research team compared the character traits to external business success data. A very common measure for business is the return on assets (ROA). Is the company becoming more or less valuable over time? The findings were astounding. Controlling only for character, we found that the top half of the study pool had an average of 5.3% ROA, while the bottom half had a 1.9% ROA. When we showed the data in quartiles, the differences were even stronger. The top 25% of CEOs had an 8.4% ROA, while the bottom 25% actually lost value (-0.6% ROA). This was probably the first data showing that character drives business results. Being a good person, forgiving yourself and others, keeping your word, taking responsibility for your actions, and caring about your team are measurably connected with business success.

A commitment to character encourages an engaged workforce. Self-focus, fear motivation, "holding feet to the fire," and grudge keeping produce a demoralized and at-best compliant workforce. When employees are in a zone of compliance, they will focus on doing what they need to do to not get in trouble. Goals and metrics end up being the ceilings of accomplishment. When employees are engaged, they look back at the goals as they blow by them. There is alignment between what is good for me and what is good for the organization.

Character is not an innate personality trait. It can be taught through practicing character habits such as empathy, moving from "me first" to "others first," and owning up to mistakes. With empirical data backing the value of character, the fundraising leader should start by thinking, "What kind of leader do I want to be?"

STUDENTS OF THE BUSINESS

Abigail Adams said, "Learning is not attained by chance; it must be sought for with ardor and attended to with diligence." When you rise to a leadership position, you have not completed your journey. You've only begun the next leg. This is not the time to rest on your laurels. This is the time to seek how you can accomplish even more.

Over the years I have been invited to speak at several graduate program classes, ranging from nonprofit management and fundraising to data science and economics. When I meet with the aspiring data scientists, I will invariably receive the same questions. Students will ask if they should focus more on R or Python for data analysis. Should they immerse themselves in deep learning? Which skills and techniques look the best to future employers? My answer is always the same. I've seen both brilliant data scientists fail to make an impact and turnover quickly and average data sciences transform an institution. The difference is the domain knowledge. I tell them, "Decide what field you wish to apply your data science skills to and become a nerd about it." If they want to become a fundraising data scientist, it is more impressive to the hiring manager to say, "I've studied fundraising thoroughly. I think there are five key ways it could be better. Let me show you some of the ways I can help make that happen."

Learn about the business of fundraising. Why is encouraging major gift officers to go on discovery calls an issue at every institution? Perhaps there are learnings from behavioral economics, psychology, or related sales that could help lead to a solution. Why do we continue to have such an extensive talent gap? Is the supply and demand imbalance, which invariably leads to increased transiency and wage inflation, sustainable? What could we do to combat this trend at my institution? If our major gift business model leverages annual giving to build our base of future major donors, why is our primary metric for the annual giving team alumni participation instead of increased lifetime value and high-wealth sourcing?

If you have reached this point in the book, I realize you are a learner. Books are an effective way to open your mind to new ideas. There are many more ways you can advance your skills. Conferences are great and can help make new connections and get a pulse on the industry. Sometimes it is more effective to go on a site visit and really dig into the details with an industry peer or aspirant peer. Consider coursework on organizational management or leadership. Find a mentor and meet regularly. Offer to be a mentor and learn from the questions you get. Offer to speak at a conference to crystallize your thinking on a topic. Certainly, the ideas are numerous.

EMBRACING FUNDAMENTALS

Throughout the book you've read my opinions about best practices. Too often, best practices are code words for being like everyone else. Maybe you've jumped to the conclusion that I do not value the fundamentals of the business. Quite the contrary, a jazz musician can't improvise until she learns the chords. Your organization may not be able to embrace the new unless it gets some key functions working consistently.

As a fundraising leader, you should regularly evaluate your programs, whether using internal resources or by paying an evaluator. This will help you establish baselines to determine areas of risk or opportunity.

When you have a physical, the doctor will order a series of lab reports. These reports will show results of blood analysis in areas of cholesterol, blood sugar, liver counts, and so on. The first time you have it done, you will see your counts in the context of the normal ranges. If your numbers are in that range, you have nothing to worry about. If your numbers deviate from the range, you will have context for your next conversation with your doctor. If you have regular physicals, in addition to the context of normal ranges, the doctor will show your progression over time. Are counts improving? Are counts getting worse?

An outside evaluator, like the physician, will have the context of what's normal in your program and provide some context. If you continue to evaluate regularly against your baselines, you will begin to see if things are improving or going the other way.

Another principle for solidifying fundamentals is establishing sound management practices. As leaders, we often look outside of organizations, but we need to look within at times. One method I find very helpful is establishing guiding principles. If you've read Ray Dalio, the Heath Brothers, or the Navy's KISS principle (Keep It Simple, Stupid), you realize providing straightforward frameworks for decision-making will help your middle managers and staff make decisions. In Chapter 4, I described the three guiding principles for my company. Here they are with a little bit more detail.

1. *Advance.* We are a mission-driven for-profit organization. All our work and our research should advance the charitable sector, advance our clients' success, and advance our ability to make lasting impact.

2. *Discover.* Our goal is to identify, align, or invent which practices are best for our clients to be successful. Our discovery of these next practices is collaborative with each other, with our clients, and with the sector.

3. *Thrive.* All BWF employees should commit to a thriving work environment where all people, regardless of role, race, personal expression, or ability are valued. We will lift each other up through mistakes and support each other in failures. In our pursuit to be the best place to serve nonprofits, we are committed to the character traits of compassion, forgiveness, integrity, and responsibility.

I can't be involved in every decision. I shouldn't be involved in every decision. The same is true of our senior leadership team. By outlining the guiding principles for how we make decisions, the whole company has a mirror to hold up against new initiatives, business decisions, and client decisions. Does this idea actually help our clients, or does it only help us? Are we rehashing what has been done or working collaboratively for what should be done? Will pursuing this idea threaten an inclusive and thriving work environment?

PURSUING THE EDGE

Innovation is my hands-down favorite part of leadership. Maybe it's the composer in me. Or maybe it's my assortment of Gallup *StrengthsFinder* traits (Futurist, Ideation, Intellection, Strategic, Self-Assurance). I just love to create things that never existed before to make people happy and provide true value. As expectations for funds continue to grow and our organizations become more complex, we all need to push ahead into the unknown.

Normally, innovation is the result of applying a concept from one context into another. In my early years when still doing data science, I mostly pulled from other industries. Lending had a close equivalent to prospect research in their underwriting departments. Underwriters study capacity and propensity to make loans. The pre-underwriting step of running a credit score was the early prototype for building major gift models. Copying the approach exactly failed miserably at first. The top predictor of paying back a loan was a history of paying back loans. When prospecting for new major donors, using a history of major giving only produced people we already had identified. We had to look for methods of predicting a behavior for a statistically anomalous group before the behavior happens. The closest example I found at the time was fraud detection. Although fraud was a negative deviance event and major giving is a positive deviance event, both are effective for finding distinguishing change within messy and missing data.

There are many examples of the fundraising profession improving by adapting methods used in other sectors. Prospect relationship management liberally pulls from sales pipeline management. The dynamic scoring methods Amy and I developed for the arts were inspired by dynamic ticket pricing. Expanded blending of complex assets to fund principal gifts is quite similar to the creative structuring used in mergers and acquisitions. Some of the most effective ask arrays in direct response leverage anchor-pricing strategies used in retail. Think of the donor welcome pack used by donor relations departments in response to a donor's first-ever gift. This is an adaptation of the customer delight concept.

Customer delight is surprising a customer by exceeding their expectations and thus creating a positive emotional reaction:

1. Make customers loyal. Finding new customers costs four to nine times more time and money than reselling to an existing client. It is thus commercially intelligent to retain as many clients as possible.

2. Have customers that are more profitable. Average delighted customers spend more with less hassle. When all other elements are correct, clients accord less importance to price (as long as their perception of price remains reasonable).

3. Have clients talk positively about your product, brand, or shop, the so-called word of mouth. In a world of informed customers, 92% of customers consider word of mouth as the most reliable source of information. Delighted clients can be a valuable source of advertisement for a company. (Wikipedia, 2019)

Some innovations are unique to our industry. For example, commitment-based counting, deferred-giving instruments, and campaign volunteer structures are rather unique to fundraising. Regardless of the source and context, fundraising leaders set out to try something new to either solve an existing problem or open the door to a new opportunity.

Rutgers University's increasingly innovative fundraising program under Nevin Kessler's leadership and Jessica Miller's innovative thinking created a new method of determining campaign themes and priorities. They assembled and refined gift ideas from around campus, gathered a couple of hundred donors to campus, and used a *Shark Tank*-type approach to present the ideas to donors. They received direct feedback on what was compelling and feasible for their campaign in a completely new way.

My BWF colleague Bond Lammey, while in a previous role as director of prospect research for the University of Chicago, created a single-source rating methodology to the time-consuming verification process. Researchers were now able to vet screening results and referrals to pass forward to major gift officers in a fraction of the time it takes for most research departments.

Marianne Haggerty of Caltech collaborated with me to create a cross-corroborating screening algorithm. By conducting regression analysis of screening results by multiple companies, weighting each component at the asset level, and building a new capacity calculation, we were able to increase accuracy of ratings by 70%.

Similar to establishing guiding principles for managing fundamentals, I find it effective to create an expanded innovation rubric to serve as a test for new ideas. Here is a sample rubric:

Benefits

1. Does the potential innovation enhance an existing capability at our organization? In other words, does it make something we already do better or more efficient?
2. By pursuing this idea, would we be able to offer a more valuable service to our donors?

3. Would it benefit multiple areas of our program?
4. Will we see more gifts, higher lifetime value, or bigger gifts?
5. Is it aligned to our organization's guiding principles?

Risks

1. If we do this, could there be an adverse effect in giving?
2. Will the quality of work be to the expectations of our brand identify?
3. Is the cost higher than the potential benefit?
4. Will there be an operational impact that taxes our existing staff unreasonably?

In Chapter 2, I described how innovation flows out of a forgiving culture. It is necessary to understand that most ideas will not come to fruition in the ways you expect, if they succeed at all. You will fail often. The resolve to continue pursuing the edge will make you a stronger leader and may produce the next great idea. Give yourself and your team room for what's next.

MODELING EXCELLENCE

Over the years I've come to realize a truth I first heard in a Manager Tools podcast (www.manager-tools.com) years ago. When you become the boss, it is as though there is a giant neon sign over your head wherever you go saying, "The Boss." The energy changes when you enter the room. As much as you try and make friends with your employees and pursue a universally valued and inclusive environment, they will always recognize the role differential. But they will also learn from your example.

Ralph Waldo Emerson said, "An Institution is the lengthened shadow of one man." Although I do not like the gender-specific nature of the quote, I think Emerson has a point. The institution reflects the personality of its leader. If the leader values compassion, the organization will begin to value compassion. If the leader is driven by fear, the organization will respond to this fear with CYA language, blame, and gatekeeper dependence. If the leader models excellence, the program will become excellent.

This is a tremendous responsibility for the fundraising leader. You set the tone for the organization by your own behaviors. To build the organization your mission and your donors deserve, focus on being the leader your mission and your donors deserve. Your organization will follow your example.

Manager of the Fundraising Business

Like fundraising, leadership is not a new concept. However, I have found that in many instances fundraising leaders are not given the adequate tools for successfully managing and leading a team without being thrown into the deep end first. Like our profession of fundraising, we as development professionals many times "fall into" management and leadership as well. It happens often in one of two scenarios:

Scenario 1
A fundraiser rises up through the ranks of their team, being given progressively increased responsibilities based on their previous performance. They have exceeded revenue goals and proven capable of handling more.

Perhaps they started in gift processing, then moved to the annual fund, then individual giving and finally major gifts. They were given more responsibility as they were able to accomplish and excel in their current duties. Next, they moved to major gifts, and then, after exceeding revenue goals as an officer, they are given staff to manage.

Along this particular career journey, the fundraiser is sometimes given the tools for success of managing a team, but I'm afraid that is not always the case. Rarely are their managerial or leadership qualities accessed to see if they would make a good team leader. In my experience, some officers should never have a direct report and are far more productive as gift officers. In fact, the more staff you manage, the less productive you personally are as a revenue producer. You have to balance bringing in major gift revenue as well as managing people. I once asked Josh how many direct reports a fundraising manager should have, based on research. It's recommended that one should not manage more than *five to six direct reports*, otherwise you are spending all your time managing a team instead of achieving fundraising goals. I have managed fundraising teams for over a decade, and it is still a struggle to juggle and balance all the balls of the fundraising business.

The Peter Principle states that "good rule followers get promoted by management until they become bad leaders." There is very little research to show how the Peter Principle applies to fundraising, but we can see a correlation with our colleagues in sales. Sales employees actually decreased their revenue and productivity the moment they became managers. The high-revenue-producing salespeople increased their chances of earning a promotion by about 14% each time they doubled their sales. Firms would prioritize "current job performance in promotion decisions at the expense of other observable characteristics that better predict managerial performance." Sales declined an average of 7.5% on teams led by managers who had doubled sales when they were just in charge of themselves ("Promotions and the Peter Principle," National Bureau of Economic Research, 2018).

Our fundraising profession needs to take a hard look at who we are promoting in our field and why they are being promoted. Some of the best major gift officers should stay as officers and not be given teams to lead. Other staff members may exhibit excellent leadership skills but not be the highest revenue producers, and therefore great candidates for management. This is why talent management is a critical new focus for the development profession, more on that topic can be found later in the chapter.

Scenario 2

Fundraisers get overlooked for promotions within their current organization, so they look for (one of many) open job opportunities that will provide increased responsibilities and perhaps a management position elsewhere. They leave their current positions and take a role at a new organization. They may have three to five years of fundraising experience under their belts, but this new position is the first time they have managed a team, with little to no prior management experience.

This was my experience. I had left my prior position to gain board and major gifts experience and was very fortunate to be handed the reins to lead my first fundraising team in my late 20s. I had been in development for six years and was ready for a new challenge, so I took my first director of development position leading a small team for an education nonprofit in 2008 (during the financial recession). It was tough, but I am still so proud we exceeded our goal that year. I was truly grateful for this position, but talk about a crash course in management! Luckily, I had colleagues and my mentor Dorothy along the way to help me navigate this unchartered territory, but it wasn't until five years later that I was sent to a formal management training course. We need to be empowering our fundraisers with management courses and training sessions, not only to help them advance their careers, but to help with retention. Don't fall into the trap of giving a young ambitious employee an intern to manage. Train them and teach them the ways of managing employees. If you are a member of senior leadership, set them up with a mentor in the management team to learn about how to manage a team. You will not only empower current employees and future leaders, but their future employees will thank you.

FUNDRAISING MANAGER VERSUS LEADER

The reason I differentiate between the leader from the manager in the development business is that these are two separate types of supervisors. Development leaders are much harder to find in our profession. We can characterize the fundraising manager as the head of a team or department who tends to focus on tasks and processes at hand. There is a focus on the details instead of bigger picture or strategy. Managers are critically important in implementing processes, efficiencies, and protocols, but I would not suggest they lead an entire department unless they exhibit leadership qualities.

Here is how you might distinguish between these two types of roles:

1. *Leaders* set the vision and direction for the team in accordance with the mission of the organization. They provide guiding principles for the team and institution. Leaders model culture expectations for their team. Leaders care deeply about the team and the organization.

2. *Managers* are excellent at converting vision into action. They provide decision-making frameworks so their teams can move forward on projects and help solve problems. Managers model culture expectations for their teams. They too care deeply about the team and the organization.

Both leaders and managers are essential to the function and process of an advancement or development department. However, I think it is crucial for a chief development officer or director of development to be a fundraising leader to establish the vision and culture of the team and strategically guide them into the future.

LEADERSHIP CHARACTERISTICS

In the following list, I have included some leadership qualities or character traits I have identified and witnessed during my tenure as a fundraiser. These character traits can be innate or learned. Either way, the fundraising leader must have a desire to grow these characteristics along their career journey:

- *Collaboration:* The more leaders provide exposure to collaborating across fundraisers and programs within an organization, the better it is for all. In sales, for example, it was once measured that "the number of colleagues with whom a worker shared credit on transactions" had increased sales by 30% for their teams.

- *Vision:* Fundraising leaders have the passion and vision to chart the course ahead for their teams and see where the teams need to go three to five years down the road. They should be able to build their teams around mission, values, strategic plans and benchmarks established by the organization and in accordance with metrics from similar types of other organizations.

- *Innovation:* Fundraising leaders are constantly looking toward next practices to advance their teams and, if feasible, their sector and industry. Regardless of the size of their teams, the leader trains, educates, and casts a vision for what their teams are able to achieve.

- *Humility:* Fundraising leaders are able to admit their mistakes, say they are sorry, confess when they don't know the answer, or ask for help or more information. A fundraising leader knows how to delicately guide themselves and their staff through "failing well." They credit the team more than themselves and serve the team as servant leaders fighting against pride, arrogance, or egotism. To quote the late Kobe Bryant, "Serve, don't lead."

- *Responsibility:* Leaders take the weight of their position very seriously and know when to stand up for themselves and their teams. They wear their title with confidence and reverence, knowing they are representing the organization in the community.

- *Advocacy:* Fundraising leaders advocate for their colleagues in the field externally from the organization, and internally to their organization they advocate for their teams/direct reports. They advocate for fair and equitable compensation for themselves and for their teams. They advocate for their organizations with their cities and communities.

- *Inspiration:* Fundraising leaders empower their teams and peers toward greatness and their ultimate potential. They expose colleagues to new ideas and thoughts, so collectively they can advance the field together.

- *Ethical:* Leaders seek to pursue and lead their teams with the highest of ethical standards.

- *Discretion:* Fundraising leaders are exposed to confidential information constantly before their teams are privy to it. They can control messaging and know when information should or should not be communicated to their teams.

- *Perseverance:* Fundraising leaders have "grit." They have the determination and endurance to hit their goals and achieve what is needed for their organization. They persevere in their current position for as long as possible.

- *Patience:* Fundraising leaders realize they must commit to endurance and patience with themselves, their organizations, and their teams.

- *Balance:* Fundraising leaders understand that balance between home and work is crucial for maintaining a career in the field. The lives of fundraisers can be all encompassing unless balance is thoughtfully achieved.

BUILDING A TEAM

As a leader, it is critical to find the right person and fit for the team and organization, otherwise it leads to a strained and contentious work environment. Finding the right team member is always worth the wait. Whenever I started with a new organization, I assessed the team's strengths and weakness by listening and observing. I then looked at opportunities to reorganize and create stronger and more efficient processes, taking into account team dynamics. I started by raising the bar of expectations for what needed to be accomplished, then I challenged the team to adopt new and future practices. It usually took a couple of years to accomplish, but by then, the team was operating with greater efficiency and camaraderie.

STAFF RETENTION

According to *The Chronicle of Philanthropy*, 51% of development professionals planned to leave their current positions in 2021. Many plan to leave the profession all together (Heather Joslyn, "51% of Fundraisers Plan to Leave Their Jobs by 2021, Says New Survey," *The Chronicle of Philanthropy*, August 6, 2019).

We are in a major fundraising shortage at this time, which has gotten worse during the pandemic due to staff attrition, and it will become a development staffing crisis if we don't act now. It takes a development officer six to eight months to start producing results. It takes a chief development officer eight months or more to ramp up operations. Therefore, it is imperative for nonprofits to retain their fundraising staff and set them up for success. Fundraising managers must advocate and adapt to their staff needs to retain their high-performing staff. Investment in professional development activities, team lunches or happy hours, and staff birthday and anniversary celebrations does not have to cost a lot of money and leads to the direct retention of your employees. As leaders, we must adapt to the changing landscape of the fundraising workforce, including remote working options for employees, to stay competitive.

Especially with so many women and parents in our field, retention also looks like flexible work schedules. A previous supervisor and friend comments how she learned about leading team members who were parents when we worked together. I was able to provide real-time experience and empathy of how to handle various parent commitments or situations. In my past two positions, ironically enough, we would experience a baby boom with my employees. A couple of employees commented to me before going on maternity leave that I gave them hope that one could balance being a mom and a fundraising professional. It is hard, but it is possible! Fundraising leaders now must understand the rhythm of parenting in order to accommodate a dual workforce. I have managed mothers, grandmothers, and fathers, and the key is flexibility, communication, and accountability. If a kid is sick at home and someone can perform their job from home that day, give that team member the flexibility to do so. They'll likely be grateful for that gesture. Sometimes employees must run their children to doctor appointments or attend parent teacher conferences, but they are still able to accomplish the work that is needed that week. I found that the key to higher retention is to establish strong communication with my teams but give them the flexibility they need. Corporations are implementing this kind of flexibility for parents in their workforces especially with virtual work options available if we want lower staff attrition, nonprofits need to adapt as well.

PROFESSIONAL DEVELOPMENT

It was always important to me to provide my staff with professional development opportunities because it helped retain them. Such opportunities not only help your team members become better fundraisers but also challenge them to keep learning and growing in the field. They provide networking opportunities and can spark your team to continue to pursue a career in fundraising. You can also look at internal cross-training as a professional opportunity for staff to understand another part of the business and to share their expertise. You need to create professional development opportunities for yourself to grow as well. If you stop growing in your career, then you become an apathetic and lethargic manager. The fundraising leader cultivates future fundraisers. Lead by example by encouraging your team to have the same thirst for knowledge that you do.

To retain and prepare our managers, we must go beyond spending funds on professional development opportunities for our teams and invest in formal leadership and talent management training for fundraisers, just as corporations do for their employees. We also need to give the fundraising teams the resources they need to adequately sustain and grow operations. When fundraising leaders have the resources needed for their teams to be successful, our organizations don't just survive, they also thrive. When we invest in the nonprofit fundraising workforce, the organization and, therefore, the entire nonprofit community benefits from the success of the development team.

EMPLOYEE SATISFACTION AND ENGAGEMENT

As my colleague Alex Oftelie says, satisfaction and engagement are like cousins. Just because you have a good experience at a store and are satisfied, it does not determine your loyalty or how engaged you are with the store's brand. Brand loyalty and engagement with an institution are developed over time with thought, strategy, and intentional leadership. Likewise, for development staff members, employee satisfaction and engagement are vastly different in determining the tenure or success of employees. As addressed in Chapter 4, dispassionate employees have drastic effects on their ability to fundraise or continue to serve an institution. Thus, you see high turnover of development employees going from passion project to passion project. It is very hard for fundraisers who are honest with themselves to do their jobs effectively if they are not engaged with their nonprofit.

If employee satisfaction and engagement are cousins, then employee engagement and passion are siblings. Passion cannot exist without engagement. It is very hard to be passionate about something, including your current fundraising position, and not to be engaged.

To know how to cultivate employee engagement, we must first learn the difference between *employee satisfaction* versus *employee engagement.* As my colleague Betsy Rigby, who specializes in talent management, writes "Employee satisfaction is the extent to which employees are happy or content with their jobs and work environment. Employee engagement is the extent to which employees feel passionate about their jobs, are committed to the organization, and put discretionary effort into their work. 'Organizations with genuinely engaged employees have higher retention, productivity, customer satisfaction, innovation, and quality. They also require less training time, experience less illness, and have fewer accidents'" (Charles Rogel, "Podcast: 2018 Employee Engagement Driver Benchmark Results," Decision-wise.com, 2018).

If managers cultivate employee engagement versus satisfaction, there should be less attrition within our fundraising teams, beyond the 18–24 months that has unfortunately become the norm for our sector. Fundraising managers and leaders must proactively identify whether their employees are satisfied and engaged and determine strategies to mitigate attrition in our workforce.

CHAPTER DISCUSSION GUIDE

- Pick three leadership traits you would like to strengthen for yourself over the next year. How do you intend to accomplish that?
- If you are a supervisor, which scenario applies most to you and why?
- What are ways you can help with staff retention on your team?
- Write down two professional development opportunities you plan to pursue in the next year.

CLOSING

When I first started fundraising more than 20 years ago, I had a perception of what I thought fundraising was. The majority of people in the field fall into it and then realize we have a passion for it. For me, I was fresh out of acting conservatory and, because the lifestyle and career of a professional actor is incredibly difficult, I heeded the words of my professor: "If you can do anything else besides perform, then do it." I was first exposed to fundraising at a theater company in California that took a chance and hired me as the development associate. Other applicants had more experience than I did, but I was a known entity having worked for them as an intern the previous summer.

Now, having spent my entire career in fundraising, I know our field is so much more than the superficial assumptions others make about our profession. As fundraisers, we don't just put on events. We don't just ask people for money. Fundraising is not just a job or a paycheck; it is a passion, a craft, a higher calling. Twenty years ago, I came to see fundraisers as the heartbeat of their organizations. Fundraising makes the art happen on the stage, advances medicine, provides brighter futures for students, places children into foster homes, makes our parks and cities more beautiful and our earth more sustainable, provides critical services for those in need, and makes the world a better place, all through the incredible power of philanthropy.

During my career fundraising for several types of organizations, I learned from my own experiences and from my colleagues in the industry that this business is really tough because you must be all things to all people. When trying to explain to those in the for-profit industry what I did for a living, I say development is a cross between community relations, public relations, business development, sales, investor relations, human resources, facilities, finance, marketing, and communications. Fundraisers must be a jack- or jane-of-all-trades knowing a little bit about a lot of things. Hopefully this book gave you a sense of the components or traits that make up the modern fundraiser.

During challenging and unpredictable times, it is more important than ever for us to encourage each other as development professionals to stay the course, mentor and recruit others to our field, and create a diverse and inclusive sector so people from all backgrounds and demographics can pursue this profession. With rising pressures across all sectors demanding that fundraisers raise more revenue with fewer resources, it is imperative that we band together as modern fundraisers to strive for these traits and avoid burnout.

Amidst the Great Resignation, we are experiencing a nation-wide shortage of qualified development professionals ready to lead the nonprofit industry and willing to stay in their positions for a substantial period of time. How can we collectively create a "farm team" of fundraising talent to help feed the pipeline of nonprofit leaders who will build a sustainable philanthropic sector of the future? This talent gap is a perennial challenge to the fundraising profession, and it is exacerbated by increased retirements, job changes, and jumping organizations. This is why Josh and I felt a sense of urgency to write this book now. In collaboration, our hope was to articulate how imperative it is that modern fundraisers understand how to survive, grow, and thrive to lead successful teams and organizations of the future.

May this book be a practical and tactical guide for you in your career or for your fundraising or advancement teams to help advance their craft. Perhaps this book can be the introduction for conversations with your executive leaders or teams about what fundraising is and is not. Maybe this book will provide validation that you are on the right path within your current position, reignite a passion in you about why you pursued this profession in the first place, or give you a better understanding about starting a career in this noble profession. Please feel free to read this book in its entirety or break it down into chapters, using the questions at the end of each chapter to facilitate discussions with your team, with a mentor, or with a "development circle"—a group of trusted colleagues in the field.

Our sincere desire is for this book to shed light on what we can do to stay ahead of the curve so that we as fundraisers and our organizations don't just survive but thrive. This book is meant to be a catalyst for conversations and reflections so that fundraisers can band together to advance our field, encourage our colleagues to persevere within their current positions, and recruit the next generation of fundraisers.

Thank you so much for joining us for this journey and taking the time to read our stories.

—Amy Lampi

INDEX